Steps in Ballet

Basic Exercises at the Barre

Basic Center Exercises

Basic Allegro Steps

Steps in Ballet

Basic Exercises at the Barre
Basic Center Exercises
Basic Allegro Steps

Thalia Mara

Princeton Book Company, Publishers

Steps in Ballet combines three separate books by Thalia Mara in one volume:
First Steps in Ballet: Basic Exercises at the Barre,
Second Steps in Ballet: Basic Center Exercises,
and *Third Steps in Ballet: Basic Allegro Steps.*

Princeton Book Company, Publishers
P.O. Box 831
Hightstown, NJ 08520-0831

Design and composition by Lisa Denham

Library of Congress Cataloging in Publication Data
Mara, Thalia.
    Steps in ballet: basic exercises at the barre, basic center exercises, basic allegro steps / Thalia Mara.
    p. cm.
        ISBN 0-87127-262-8

    1. Ballet

                                                        RA645.6.N7R45 2003
                                                        362.18'092'297471—dc21

2003044884

Printed in Canada   6, 5, 4, 3, 2, 1

Contents

Foreword: To Parents

This book, while explicit in details and analysis of basic ballet barre exercises, is not intended as a guide to self-instruction. *It has been written as an aid to intelligent practice at home for the ballet student.* As such I believe that it meets a genuine need and demand.

The study of ballet should be undertaken only under the expert guidance of a really competent teacher. Even if these exercises seem very clear to you or your child I strongly urge against self-instruction. The bones of a young child are soft and malleable. The tendons and muscles of the feet and legs interlace with those of the back and it is the correct use of these tendons and muscles pulling against each other which build the strength and shapeliness of the ballet dance. A good teacher knows all of these things and how to balance the exercises to develop the results of grace, beauty, and poise. Incorrect repetition of the details of these same exercises can have a disastrous effect on the feet, back, and muscular development of the legs.

CHOOSING A TEACHER

For these reasons I urgently advise you to be certain that your child is studying under a *bona fide* teacher of ballet—one who understands the principles of body placement, who knows the correct balance of the basic exercises of ballet and carefully supervises their correct execution by the individual student in the class.

If you are in doubt as to how to choose a teacher with proper qualifications, be guided by the answers to these questions:

WHAT IS THE TEACHER'S BACKGROUND? It should include at least four or five years of intensive and concentrated study under a recognized ballet master. Professional experience does not always mean that the teacher is an expert on ballet. There are many kinds of dancing in the professional theater. If your teacher's background includes performing in a ballet company, you are very fortunate, as this experience will aid in developing artistry in your child. However, a teacher with a good solid background of earnest study under recognized ballet masters is preferable to one who may have had years of theatrical experience but little training in the fundamentals of ballet technique. While there are many good ballet teachers who belong to organizations of dancing teachers, membership in such an organization does not necessarily mean that the teacher is qualified to teach ballet.

WHAT DOES THE TEACHER CLAIM TO TEACH? Today "ballet" is a magic word—one that spells glamour and beauty to hundreds of thousands of little girls and their parents. If your child is studying ballet because you wish her to have the advantages of increased grace, poise, beauty of posture, and sound, symmetrical muscular development, then what you want her to have is *academic classical ballet technique.*

DOES THE TEACHER ACCEPT CHILDREN OF ANY AGE FOR BALLET TRAINING? Ballet experts everywhere agree that children under eight years of age should not begin physical training in ballet. The reasons for this are both physical and psychological. Of course there have been a few notable exceptions to this rule, but such exceptions are very rare. There is nothing to be gained by starting the child too soon and much may be lost.

Physically, the technical exercises of ballet, if performed correctly, are too severe for the very soft bones of children under eight years

of age. There is too much strain on the knees and the back. Mentally the child is incapable of the concentration required to understand the details of correct execution. If the exercises are performed incorrectly, permanent damage may be done to the feet and muscular structure of the legs.

There is also the danger that real talent may be destroyed by forcing the immature mind into something for which it is not ready. Ballet is a very disciplined art. While it provides an interesting and even fascinating challenge to the child old enough to appreciate and grasp its principles, such discipline is too exacting for the very young child who needs more freedom of thought and expression.

Children from four to eight years may very profitably study dancing, but it should be a form of dance based on rhythmic exercises, movements for coordination and grace, and little dances based on nursery rhymes and fairy tales. Such preballet training is an excellent preparation for the study of actual ballet technique. Under no circumstances should they permitted to dance on *pointe* (on their toes).

DOES THE TEACHER USE A GRADED SYSTEM? A really good teacher does, beginning with the most basic fundamentals and advancing by stages to more difficult exercises, steps, and combinations of steps. This system may be the teacher's own if he or she has had sufficient background and experience to evolve such a system, or it may be the system of a famous teacher or master.

There are three distinct schools of technique in ballet: the Russian, the Italian (also called Cecchetti), and the French. The teacher may base his system entirely on the theory of one school or on a combination of them. My own preference, based on my professional experiences both as a dancer and as a teacher, is for a combination of the Russian and Italian theories: the Italian to give strength, balance, and perfect coordination of the legs, arms, torso, and head; and the Russian to give grace and a larger sense of freedom in movement.

Wherever possible, when differences of opinion may exist among the various techniques, I have endeavored to explain the differences so that there will be no confusion in the student's mind. But in all cases I have set forth what in my considered opinion is the best form.

Although the art of ballet is international in scope, appeal, technique, and terminology, it takes on the national characteristics of each country in which it finds a home. Just as the Russian dancers, trained by both the French and Italian masters, adapted these techniques to suit their national temperament and characteristics, so we, in America, have been in the process of developing an American school of technique based on the traditions of all three schools.

Nobility of carriage, fluidity of body lines and poses, perfect coordination of head and arms in graceful *port de bras*—these are the marks of a good ballet dancer in every country. It is useless to become embroiled in arguments over whether an arm position is called *third* or *fourth, first* or *fifth*. What matters is that the arms are held correctly and that the hands are graceful and fluent, not ungraceful and rigid.

The art of ballet extends beyond mere movement. It fuses all of the arts, combining music, dance, design and drama. The child who is fortunate enough to study ballet will find his entire life enriched by this experience.

WHAT IS THE TEACHER'S VIEWPOINT ON "TOE DANCING?" Beware of the teacher to whom "ballet" means only toe dancing (on *pointe*). Dancing on the tips of the toes is the very ultimate in technique for the ballerina. Its study should not be begun until after at least two or three years of consistent study and practice in the basic exercises of ballet. When sufficient strength has been built in the feet, legs, and back of the child, so that she can stand on the *demi-pointes* perfectly "placed," with her knees tightly pulled up and the weight lifted up from her feet, so that her toes do not bear the dead weight of her body, then she is ready to begin dancing *sur les pointes*, or on her toes.

DOES THE TEACHER TREAT BALLET AS A SEPARATE SUBJECT? A great many teachers, particularly those in the smaller towns throughout the country, must include in the curriculum of their schools a variety of dancing such as ballet, tap, acrobatic, ballroom, jazz, or modern. There is no reason why they should not. However, tap and other types of dance must be taught in classes separate from ballet. No real teacher who knows and understands ballet will teach it in combination with other subjects—such as twenty minutes of ballet, twenty minutes of tap, and twenty minutes of acrobatic. Nothing constructive can be gained or accomplished in this manner.

A ballet class should consist entirely of ballet technique and should be one hour in length. Later, as the student advances and becomes stronger, classes may be lengthened to one and one-half hours. For children one hour is sufficient. Each class should be partitioned into *barre* work, *port de bras*, center *barre*, *adagio* and *allegro*. A beginner should spend thirty or forty minutes of the hour at the *barre* in order to acquire the placement, strength, and balance necessary to execute the center work correctly.

Don't be misled by phrases such as "modern methods" or "old-fashioned methods." This is usually a cover-up for ignorance of true methods.

The importance of the choice of a teacher cannot be overstressed. To instill a love for the arts in any child the teacher must love and respect his or her art. One must not be influenced by such considerations as cheaper lessons or convenient location. That which seems cheapest or most convenient may turn out, in the long run, to be the dearest and least convenient as the bitter price is paid in physical damage to bone and muscle structure or the ruination of a natural talent. And this is just as true for the child without professional aspirations as it is for those with professional ambitions. Every child who studies ballet, whether with the hope of a career or merely for the physical and mental benefits to be obtained, has a right to and must be taught from the highest professional standards. For it is only the scientifically correct execution of the exercises and movements of ballet that builds the beautiful, shapely body, and brings out the grace and noble poise of the dance.

THE PARENT-STUDENT-TEACHER RELATIONSHIP

Having placed your child in the school of your choice, do all you can to encourage her by taking an active interest in her work. Be sure to attend visitors' days at the school, so that she may look forward to your approval of her progress. However, do observe the good-conduct rules for parents by doing nothing to distract the child's attention from her teacher, even if she is not doing as well as you think she should. Show your respect for the teacher by allowing her or him to do the teaching and do not try to impose your ideas on how the class should be conducted.

Help your little ballerina at home by checking her practice sessions for correct posture and placement. Above all—be patient! It takes many years of effort and persistence to make a dancer and to acquire the grace and poise you long to see your child display.

True progress in ballet is made very slowly and consists not of new steps and dances but rather of repetition of the basic exercises, steps, and movements to acquire the strength, muscle tone, and correct body placement needed. By painstaking care the teacher and student together are fashioning a dance instrument just as a craftsman fashions a fine musical instrument with his tools and basic materials. Pushing a child into more advanced steps before those already taught have been properly assimilated retards true progress. The good teacher will always vary the exercises to develop mental agility in the child as well as to maintain the child's interest.

Having selected and placed your child in the school of your choice, express your confidence in the teacher by accepting her (or his) decisions as to what your child is capable of doing. The conscientious teacher deserves your confidence and support.

The conscientious teacher who is trying to help your child to better posture through the strengthening regime of exercise (for it takes a great deal of strength in the postural muscles to aid the child in standing straight) has an easier job with a child who is enthusiastic about exercise and who is physically ambitious. There are varying degrees of aptitude, too, to be considered. I use the word "aptitude" rather than "talent," for real dance talent does not begin to show until after several years of training.

Most children, even those who lack real aptitude and the physical attributes for dancing, develop a love for their lessons and enthusiasm for their work. I believe that this is caused, in large part, by the challenge that good training presents to them and to their feeling of achievement when they accomplish the mastery of a step or exercise.

BOYS IN BALLET

Although the illustrations of this book are feminine and addressed mainly to girls, I would like to point out that ballet is not just a feminine art. Actually it began as a masculine art and it is still a manly and fine art for boys in spite of the popular misconception that it is "sissy." As anyone who has seen a ballet performance knows, there is nothing more thrilling than the performance of a fine male dancer.

Ballet requires the strength of an athlete, but it is twice as difficult as athletics because the strength must be concealed by ease of movement. Many coaches are sending their basketball and football team members to ballet classes to learn coordination. Famous boxers have studied ballet to improve their footwork. It is time American boys and their parents overcome this silly attitude. Studying the arts will not make a sissy out of any boy who is not already one. If you would like your son to develop a strong, healthy body, good physical and mental coordination, an appreciation of music, painting, literature, and drama— send him to a ballet class!

BALLET DEVELOPS THE WHOLE CHILD

The habits of concentration, perseverance, and the ability to face up to challenging problems by meeting and overcoming them must be formed in childhood. One reason that exposure to ballet is so good for children is that ballet is such a highly disciplined art. The child learns to discipline both the body and the mind—something that stands us all in good stead in adult life.

Too little is done in our country to encourage a love of art in our children. Such a child finds a wonderful outlet for his emotions and energies in the inner satisfaction and genuine sense of achievement that the all-absorbing, interesting, and challenging aspects of technique and artistic expression offer. A generation of Americans raised with a love for the arts and an understanding of them will do much to enrich our country.

THALIA MARA

I

Basic Exercises at the Barre

Note To Students

If you love ballet and really want to make progress in learning its technique, you must be faithful about attending your lessons and keeping your practice schedule.

Do not miss classes for any reason except illness and do not allow anything to interfere with your practice schedule. Set aside certain hours of certain days as practice hours. Practice slowly and carefully. Each time choose one or two exercises you feel need particular attention and work to improve them.

Famous dancers who have been dancing since they were children still repeat these same barre exercises daily. If you think of all the details you are trying to get right, and of how each time you practice correctly you gain a little strength and a little ease, you will never be bored by repeating the same exercises. You can soon go on to more difficult and interesting steps.

If possible, try to have one place in which to practice. If you are lucky enough to have a playroom or a large enough bedroom, perhaps you can persuade a parent to put up a little practice barre—the wooden rail should be about 2 inches in diameter and may be secured to the wall (about 2 1/2 or 3 feet above the floor) with brackets and screws. The height of the barre depends upon your height and may be judged according to the position of your hand on the barre as in Illustration 64. If you cannot have a special barre, the footboard of your bed or the back of a chair or a stair railing will do nicely. The floor should be bare and unwaxed.

Practice for about twenty or thirty minutes each time. Of course the more often you practice the more you will improve, but you will have to work this out according to your own schedule of school, homework, playtime, dancing lessons, piano lessons.

It will inspire you to remember that every great ballerina and every great *premier danseur* in every country in the world has studied and practiced these very same exercises just as you are doing now. If you are as faithful to your work as they were, you too may reach the stars!

Posture and Placement

The very first thing a dancer must learn is how to stand properly. When we hold our bodies correctly all the steps and exercises are easier to do and they look better. In ballet we call this "correct body placement."

Remember that in practicing the exercises and steps of ballet the important thing is to practice slowly and to try to improve details. It is better to practice one thing correctly with proper attention to the details of correct placement than just to go through the motions of half a dozen exercises halfheartedly or incorrectly.

POSTURE— STAND LIKE THIS!

1   2   3   4

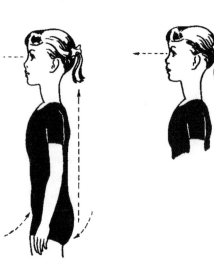

1. Pull your seat under and the stomach up so your back is flat and straight. Lift up your ribs so your chest feels high.

2. Keep your chin up and your head straight. Open your eyes and look straight out.

3. Press the shoulder blades down so your neck looks long and graceful. Allow the shoulders to remain in their natural position; don't force them back.

4. Stand with your weight forward over the balls of your feet so that your heels feel free although they remain on the floor. Try not to feel stiff, even though you feel very lifted up, breathe deeply and easily and try to feel at ease.

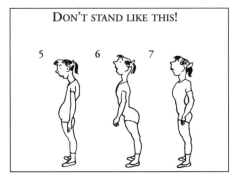

DON'T STAND LIKE THIS!

5   6   7

Correct Body Placement

Correct posture is an important part of body placement. Here are other things to remember if you want to be properly placed.

8. Lifting: lift yourself up out of your hips so your body feels as long as possible. Pull up your thigh muscles so your knees are very straight. This keeps you from being dead weight on your feet.

9. Centering: now imagine that there is a line that starts at the crown of your head and goes straight down your middle, ending between your feet. This is your "axis."

Imagine another line that goes straight across your hips. Both hips must always remain even and straight.

In everything that you do, no matter how you move, don't get off center. That is, do not allow your body to lean out of line on its axis. When you point your foot out or raise it up, be sure your hips stay in the straight line; don't let one hip get higher than the other.

8   9

DON'T DO THIS!

10   11

The Five Positions of the Feet

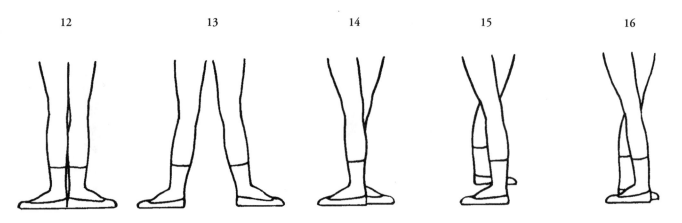

12   13   14   15   16

Here are the correct positions of the feet with the full 180° turn-out.

12. First Position: heels touching. Legs opened outward at the hip so that the feet are turned out and make a straight line from the toes of the right foot to the toes of the left foot. Both knees straight.

13. Second Position: feet are about a foot apart, weight even over both feet. Legs and feet turned outward as in First Position. Both knees straight.

14. Third Position: both legs are opened outward from the hips, and the heel of the right foot is placed in front of the arch of the left foot. The feet touch. The weight is distributed evenly over both feet. Both knees straight.

15. Fourth Position: both legs are opened outward from the hips. The feet are about one foot apart with the right foot opposite the left foot and directly in front of it (heel of the right foot in front of the toes of the left foot). Both knees straight, the weight evenly distributed over both feet.

16. Fifth Position: both legs opened outward from the hips. The heel of the right foot is in front of the joint of the big toe of the left foot. The feet touch at all points and the knees are straight. The weight is evenly distributed over both feet.

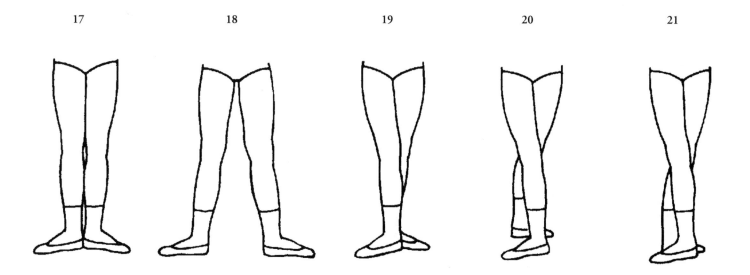

17   18   19   20   21

This full turn-out of the feet cannot be achieved immediately and if you try to force your feet to turn-out fully you will injure them. Your turn-out must come at the hip joint—the entire leg must be opened outward from the hip.

  17—21. Here are the five positions again with the right degree of turn-out for a beginner. Open your legs as far outward as your hips will allow and do not force your feet to turn out further. Turning out more than you are able from your hips is a great strain on your knees and feet. If you practice your barre exercises correctly and conscientiously, the ligaments at your hips will stretch and become limber and your turn-out will improve until you can turn your legs easily and without any strain.

22. Be sure that your foot is always straight and that all the toes are on the floor at all times. If you force your feet to turn out more than you are able to turn from the hip it will cause the feet to roll inward on the arches and can result in much damage to your feet. Be sure that as you stand, whether you are on two feet or one foot, you hold the floor firmly with the little toe and the big toe. The heel should be aligned (in line) with the toes. Grip the floor lightly with all the toes so that the instep or arch is lifted up.

22

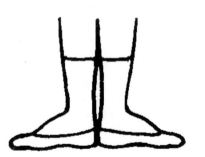

23. **DON'T DO THIS.** The little toe has been allowed to leave the floor and the foot is rolled inward.

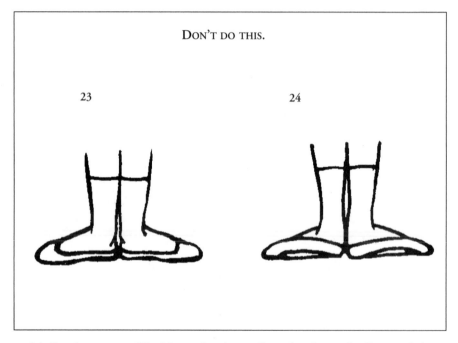

DON'T DO THIS.

23   24

24. **DON'T DO THIS.** The big toe has been allowed to leave the floor and the foot is rolling outward.

The Demi-Plié (deh'-mee plee-ay')

Your very first exercise at the barre is the *demi-plié*. It is most important for you to master this and later the *grand plié*, because the *plié* is the basis of everything you do in ballet. Practically all of the steps of ballet use the *plié* in some degree. In jumping steps it is the good *demi-plié* that gives the effect of lightness to your jumping. That is what is called *ballon*— a bouncy, light quality in all the leaping and bounding steps.

Although the *plié* may be done facing at right angle to the barre and holding it with one hand, it is a good idea to face the barre when you practice and hold it with both hands. This will help you to hold your back straight and to keep your shoulders straight front. Stand about six inches away from the barre, or at a comfortable distance so that you do not have to reach out; don't be too close, because that will make your shoulders hunch and spoil your position.

Under each set of illustrations of the *demi-plié*, in the different positions, I have given you some things to remember to do and some to remember not to do. These instructions are not just for the *demi-plié* in that particular position, but are meant for all the positions.

DEMI-PLIÉ IN FIRST POSITION

25. Ready. Bend the knees to the count.

26. "And one and two…"

27. Straighten the knees to the count "And three, and four."

The timing of the *plié* is very important. Do not bend the knees quickly and do not straighten them quickly. Take two slow counts to bend them, and then two slow counts to straighten them.

Keep the heels firmly on the floor. The *demi-plié* is especially useful to stretch the tendons at the back of the heels, so you must remember not to allow the heels to leave the floor no matter in which position you do the *demi-plié*. Keep the spine very straight, the shoulders low. Be very, very careful not to sit into your hips. Lift up out of them.

28 29 30

Demi-Plié in Second Position

28. Ready.
29. "And one, and two."
30. "And three, and four."

Remember to turn out your whole leg from the hip in all these positions. Do not force your feet to turn out further than the entire leg can turn. Keep ALL the toes on the floor, do not roll forward on your instep so that the little toe leaves the floor, and do not roll out so that the big toe leaves the floor. Hold the floor firmly with the toes so that you can feel the arches lift. Press the knees outward over the toes; do not allow them to fall forward in front of the arches.

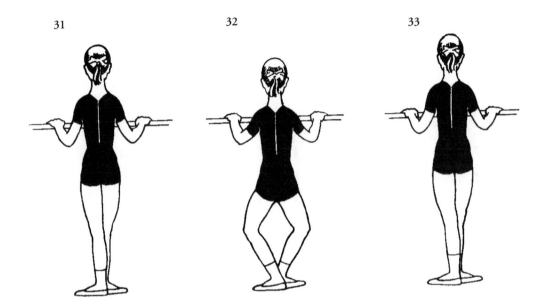

Demi-Plié in Third Position

30. Ready.
31. "And one, and two."
32. "And three, and four."

The Third Position is not often used in ballet nowadays. However, if your legs are naturally rather turned in and

you find the turn-out in Fifth Position impossible to achieve without strain and rolling in on the insteps, then practice Third Position rather than Fifth for this exercise. Proceed exactly as for Fifth Position in bending and straightening the knees.

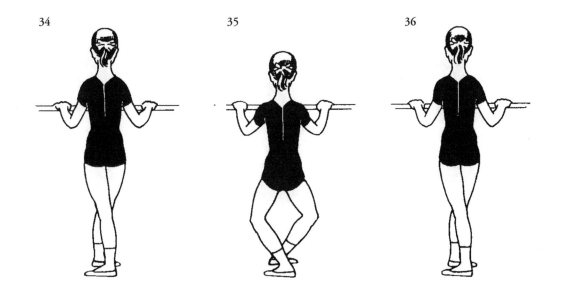

DEMI-PLIÉ IN FOURTH POSITION

34. Ready.

35. "And one, and two."

36. "And three, and four."

The Fourth Position is one of the most difficult in which to achieve a good *demi-plié*, so practice it very carefully. Be sure that both shoulders and both hips face straight front. Watch that you do not "sit " in the hip on the side of the foot which is in back. The spine must be kept straight. The foot in back will want to roll in and the knee will want to fall in front of the arch, so you must be careful not to let this happen. You can overcome this by making sure that your weight is kept even over both feet. Don't worry if you can't turn your feet outward as far as the girl in the drawing. Do the best you can correctly, and if you practice faithfully, your turn-out will improve gradually but surely.

15

37   38   39

DEMI-PLIÉ IN FIFTH POSITION

37. Ready.

38. "And one, and two."

39. "And three, and four."

We practice the *demi-plié* in order to make the muscles and ligaments of our legs very limber and supple. They must become like elastic, especially at the knees, so that they stretch and then return to their normal position readily and respond instantly when you want to move.

All ballet dancers practice their *pliés* constantly, and no professional dancer would think of beginning to practice or dance on the stage without first warming up with *plié* exercises. You must do this too.

16

The Grand Plié (grahn plee-ay')

Do not practice the *grand plié* until your teacher tells you that you do a good *demi-plié* and may now begin learning the *grand plié*. This is very important because if you cannot hold all the proper body placement in the *demi-plié* you will never be able to do the *grand plié*.

Remember not to let your seat stick out, not to sit into the hips, not to drop the ribs. The lower your knees bend, the taller you grow out of your hips, as though someone were lifting you by the crown of your head. Keep pressing your knees back and out so you feel the stretch in your hips. Watch carefully that all the toes remain on the floor even when the heels lift. Don't try to improve your turn-out by pushing your heels further front as you bend. Keep your feet in exactly the same position you had when you started.

40   41   42   43

GRAND PLIÉ IN FIRST POSITION

40.–43. Take four slow counts to bend the knees and four slow counts to straighten them.

When you allow your heels to lift off the floor, after first doing a good *demi-plié*, just allow them to raise slightly. Do not go way up on your toes. Come back up just as slowly as you went down and through the same stages, so you pass through a good *demi-plié* before your knees straighten.

Remember not to get "set" in your knees by dropping too quickly and sitting in the *plié* then jumping up too quickly. Count slowly four counts down and four counts up.

44   45   46   47

GRAND PLIÉ IN SECOND POSITION

44.–47. Take four slow counts to bend the knees, and four slow counts to straighten them.

The heel should never be allowed to leave the floor in doing the *grand plié* in Second Position. Do not bend the knees any deeper than you can while still holding a good position with everything correctly placed.

48   49   50   51

GRAND PLIÉ IN THIRD POSITION

48.–51. Take four slow counts to bend the knees, and four slow counts to straighten them.

This position need not be practiced except as a substitute for Fifth Position if that is too difficult for you at this time.

52   53   54   55

GRAND PLIÉ IN FOURTH POSITION

52.–55. Take four slow counts to bend the knees, and four slow counts to straighten them.

Take care that both knees stay at the same level all through the *plié* and both the heels are the same height off the floor. You do this by keeping your weight even over both feet. Don't let that back foot and knee roll in!

56   57   58   59

GRAND PLIÉ IN FIFTH POSITION

56.–59. Take four slow counts to bend the knees, and four slow counts to straighten them.

Be sure to keep your heels in a straight line with your toes, and as you bend keep them firmly in place, even though they lift up. Do not let your feet slip out of position so your heels turn back and your toes turn front.

60.–61. DON'T DO THIS!

60   61

Correct Position Standing at the Barre

In all the following exercises the distance between you and the barre is very important, because it has a definite effect upon your body placement as you work.

You must stand close enough to the barre to keep your hand on it slightly in front of you at all times. Your axis line (an imaginary line running from crown to toes) must always remain straight. If you are too far from the barre and have to reach for it, you will be pulled off center. If you stand too close to the barre, your arm will force your shoulder to hunch in an ugly fashion. Test this out for yourself until you find just the correct distance for comfort and good placement.

62. Too far from the barre.

63. Too close to the barre.

64. Correct position at the barre.

Position of the Free Arm and Hand at the Barre

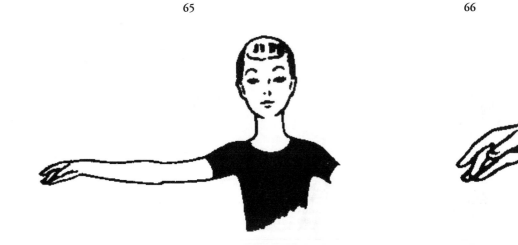

65. The arm in *seconde* position.

66. Note the grouping of the fingers. Thumb and third finger indented. When the arm is raised in Second Position, keep the elbow up and don't "break" at the wrist, but keep the hand in line with the arm.

Port de Bras at the Barre

(por deh brah)

Port de bras is the carriage of the arms. This *port de bras* at the barre is used as a preparation for *all* of the exercises that follow. It is very good to become accustomed to using the arm, and to holding it in Second Position as you work. Pay particular attention to the head, as the angle at which you hold your head is very important.

67. Stand still, ready to begin.

68. Raise the arm as high as your chest. Keep it round. Let your head incline a little toward the barre, look at the palm of your hand. Count, "And one…"

69. Open the arm to the side (Second Position). Keep the elbow lifted and slightly rounded. Follow the hand with your eyes so your head turns. Count "And two."

70. Turn your head front and look straight out, ready to begin the exercise.

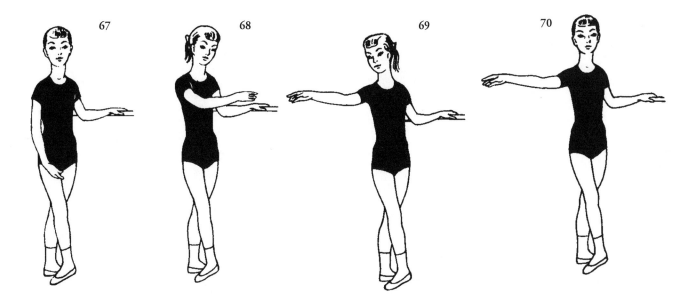

67 68 69 70

Correct Positioning of the Foot in Pointing

71. *Correct:* In pointing straight front (Fourth Position, front) try to keep the foot in its correct line with the leg, which is open (or turned out) from the hip. The heel is pressed forward and up and the point is on the big toe, not the little one.

72. *Incorrect:* Don't sickle the foot; that is, press the toes out of line with the heel.

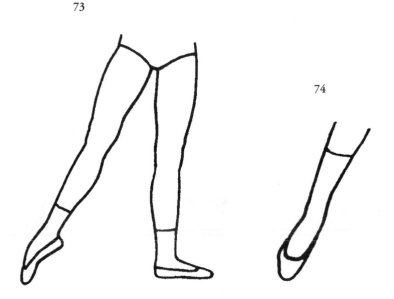

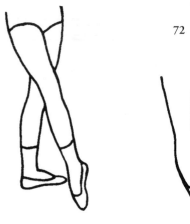

73. *Correct:* In pointing to the side (Second Position) again be sure that the foot is held in its proper alignment to the leg; that is, keep the foot on a straight line with the leg. Lift up the heel and point up on the tips of the toes.

74. *Incorrect:* Don't allow the heel to turn back.

26

75. *Incorrect:* Don't allow the heel to get out of line with the toes.

76. *Incorrect:* Don't bend your toes over to point so that you press on the knuckles.

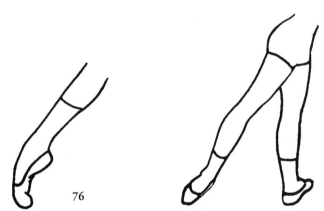

75   76   77   78

77. *Correct:* In pointing back (Fourth Position, back) rest on the inside of the big toe and press the heel down.

78. *Incorrect:* Don't turn the foot in and let the heel stick up in the air.

Battements Tendus

(baht-mahn' tahn-doo')

Every exercise you do at the barre has a special purpose. That is why it is so important to practice them correctly. If you do them only halfway, you won't get the benefits or the results you wish and expect.

Before you start each exercise take time to make sure that you are standing properly according to the principles of body placement. Test yourself to see if you are balanced forward over the balls of your feet by teetering up and down on your toes and letting go of the barre. Then put your hand back on the barre in its right place and hold the barre lightly. Be sure to stay this way all through the exercise.

Check yourself to make sure that your hips are facing straight front and are both even. See if your shoulders are both front and pressed down and relaxed.

The *battement tendu* will make your feet and legs very strong and will develop a beautiful, arched instep in your feet.

Practice it at first only from the First Position until you get the feel of it. Practice doing it *à la quatrième devant* (to the Fourth Position front), *à la seconde* (to Second Position, or side), *à la quatrième derrière* (to the Fourth Position back). As you practice, be sure your weight is centered over the ball of your supporting foot. Don't put any weight on the pointing foot.

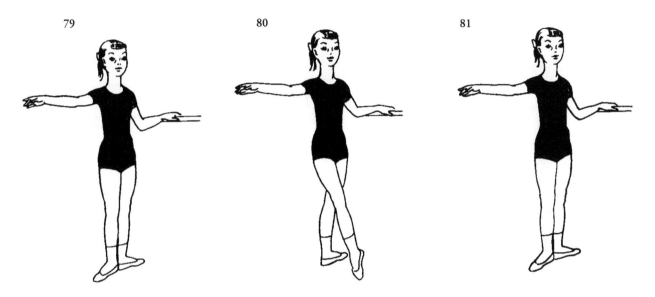

79   80   81

BATTEMENTS TENDUS À LA QUATRIÈME DEVANT
(baht-mahn' tahn-doo' ah lah caht-ree-em' deh-vahn')

Prepare with the *port de bras* as in 67 through 70.

79. Ready to begin. Left hand on barre.

80. Slide the right foot forward in a straight line as far as you can reach without getting off center or letting your right hip go forward. Keep both knees pulled up tight. Keep the heel of the pointing foot on the floor until the last possible moment so that there is a feeling of resistance in the leg as it slides out to point. Count "And one…"

81. Return the foot to First Position, sliding it back in the same manner, with the knees pulled up very tight. Be sure that your feet are not rolling in or out and that the arch of the supporting foot is lifted, because you are holding the floor firmly with ALL of your toes. Count "And two."

Practice this exercise eight times with the right foot, then turn around and do it eight times with the left foot.

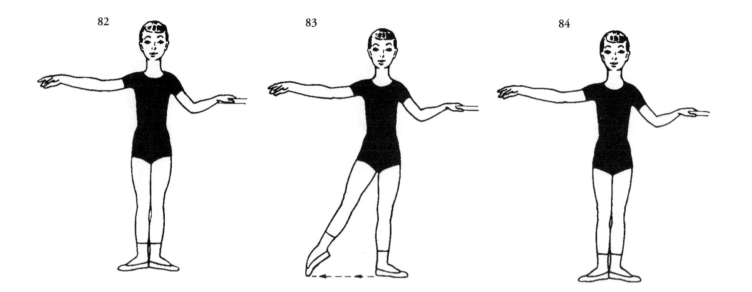

82

83

84

BATTEMENTS TENDUS À LA SECONDE
(ah lah seh-cohnd)

82. Ready.

83. "And one."

84. "And two."

This exercise is the same as *battement tendu à la quatrième devant* except that it is executed *à la seconde* (to the side). Slide the right foot out in a direct line from the left heel. Don't let the right hip raise up. Point the foot in line with the leg, heel directly under. If your seat is under and your stomach pulled up, your leg will turn out better.

30

BATTEMENTS TENDUS À LA QUATRIÈME DERRIÈRE
(ah lah caht-ree-em' dair-ee-air')

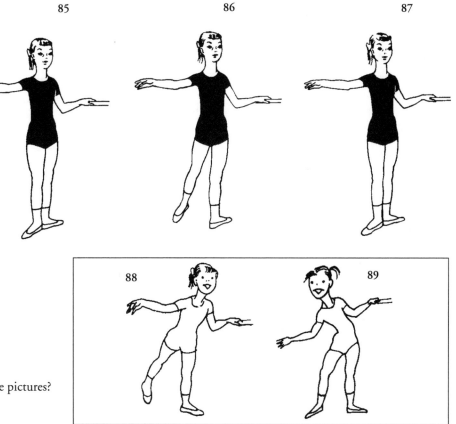

85

86

87

85. Ready.

86. "And one."

87. "And two."

Here again is the *battement tendu*, executed to Fourth Position back instead of to the front or side. Slide the right foot straight back in line with the left heel. Watch carefully that both the hips and the shoulders are facing front. Although you are trying to keep the right hip front and in line with the left hip, be careful that it does not drop forward and turn your leg in.

88

89

88.—89. What's wrong with these pictures? I hope you don't look like this!

BATTEMENTS TENDUS À LA SECONDE FROM FIFTH POSITION

When you begin to get the feel of the *battements tendus* as you practice them from First Position; that is, when you are able to slide your whole foot out till it points and slide it back to First Position again with perfectly straight knees, then you are ready to begin practicing this exercise from Fifth Position. Begin by taking it only *à la seconde* (pointing directly to the side in Second Position).

If you cannot turn your legs outward sufficiently to take Fifth Position without rolling over on your instep, practice the exercise from Third Position until your turn-out improves enough to permit a fairly good Fifth Position. Stand with your left hand on the barre, feet in Fifth Position with the right foot front. Prepare with a *port de bras* as in 67 through 70.

90. Ready to begin. Check yourself for correct posture, weight forward over the balls of the feet.

90

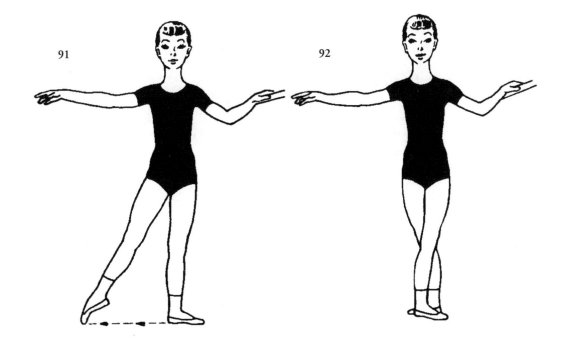

91. Count "And one…" Your toes lead out in a straight line. Remember to slide the whole foot out. The heel remains on the floor till the last possible moment.

92. Count "And two." Your heel leads in, in a straight line into Fifth Position in back of the left foot. Place the heel firmly on the floor.

Repeat the slide out to the point, then into Fifth Position, closing the left foot in front of the right foot. Repeat the entire exercise sixteen times, closing the working foot alternately in back and in front of the supporting foot. Turn around and repeat the exercise sixteen times with the left foot.

Remember not to put any weight on the pointing foot. Keep both knees pulled up tight and straight at all times. Reach out as far as you can (without getting off center) with the toes of the pointing foot.

BATTEMENTS TENDUS À LA SECONDE WITH DEMI-PLIÉ IN FIFTH POSITION

This exercise is excellent to prepare you for jumping steps so that you will have a good *ballon* or bounce in your jumping. It is done like the simple *battement tendu à la seconde*, but the knees bend outward in a *demi-plié* each time the foot closes to Fifth Position. When you are able to do this correctly pointing *à la seconde*, you may also practice it pointing *à la quatrième devant* and *à la quatrième derrière*.

Begin by standing at the proper distance from the barre, left hand on the barre, feet in Fifth Position with the right foot front. Prepare with a *port de bras* as in 67 through 70.

93. Slide the right foot out to point in Second Position. Count "And one..." Both knees are pulled up so tightly that they are very straight. (pictured on next page)

34

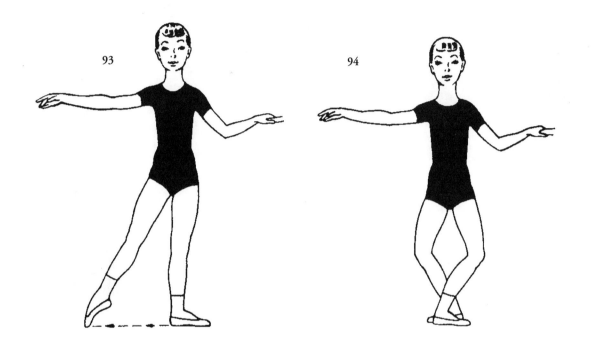

94. Slide the right foot into Fifth Position behind the left foot. As you slide the right foot in, bend both knees slowly so that when you arrive in Fifth Position both knees are bent in a *demi-plié*. Count "And two."

Take care not to roll in on your insteps. Keep the little toes firmly on the floor; both heels must be kept very straight and the body lifted up out of the hips; keep the knees directly over the toes.

Straighten both knees slowly, at the same time, as you slide the right foot out to point again in Second Position, so that when you arrive at the pointed position both knees are pulled up tight.

Practice this exercise sixteen times with each foot.

Battements Dégagés
(baht-mahn' day-gah-zhay')

95

This exercise will make your ankles very supple and will develop speed in your feet so that when you jump your feet will always be pointed beautifully. It is also important because it forms part of jumping steps such as *sissonne*, which you will learn later as you advance in ballet technique, and because it will help you in *batterie*, or beaten steps, which are part of advanced *allegro* work.

Work slowly and carefully as you practice it now.

95. Ready. Stand in First Position with the left hand on the barre. Check yourself for correct posture and good placement. Have the right arm curved and held down in front of you. Keep it there during the exercise. Incline your head slightly to the right shoulder and leave it there through the exercise.

96. Slide the entire right foot out as in *battement tendu,* but as you point the foot allow the toes to raise up off the floor about three inches. Point very strongly. Count "And one…" (pictured on next page)

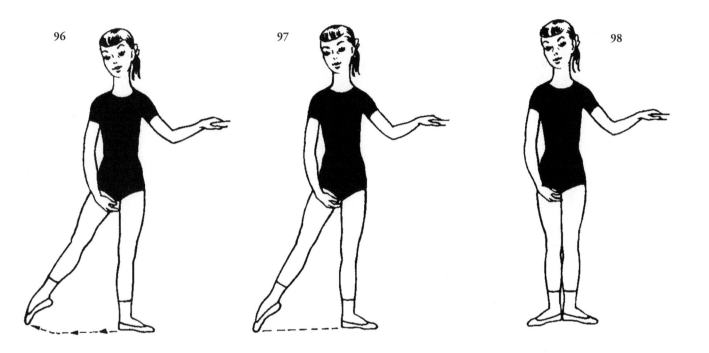

97. Lower the toes of the right foot to the floor in Second Position. Count "And two…"

98. Slide the right foot on the floor into perfect First Position. Count "And three…" Hold First Position for count "And four."

These four counts comprise the exercise. Repeat it sixteen times with each foot.

Ronds de Jambe à Terre, en Dehors

(rawn deh zhamb ah tair, ahn deh-or')

This exercise will do more than any other to loosen and limber your hip ligaments so that your turn-out will improve and your legs will become more free so that you can raise them more easily and higher off the floor.

As in all the exercises, you must stand absolutely still with the weight of the body over the ball of the supporting foot. As the working leg describes the semicircle, do not turn your hips or shoulders. Keep them facing straight front at all times.

Stand at the correct distance from the barre. Left hand on the barre, feet in First Position. Prepare with a *port de bras* as in 67 through 70.

99

100

99. Ready to begin. Perfect posture and placement, head erect, eyes looking straight forward.

100. Slide the right foot front to point in Fourth Position, as in *battement tendu*. Point the foot very strongly and keep the heel forward and up. Count "And one…"

101. Slide the toes of the right foot around on the floor to point in Second Position. Keep the foot straight as you point. Count "And two…" (pictured on next page)

102. Slide the toes of the right foot around on the floor to point in Fourth Position back. Remember to rest on the inside of the big toe with the heel pressed down. Count "And three…"

103. Slide the right foot on the floor into perfect First Position. Be careful to straighten the foot so that the little toe and the big toe are both on the floor as the foot slides in. Count "And four."

Repeat the entire exercise eight times with each foot. Work slowly, pausing in each position so that your placement through the hips will be correct and your foot positions will be turned out with the foot properly aligned to the leg. (See 71 through 73.)

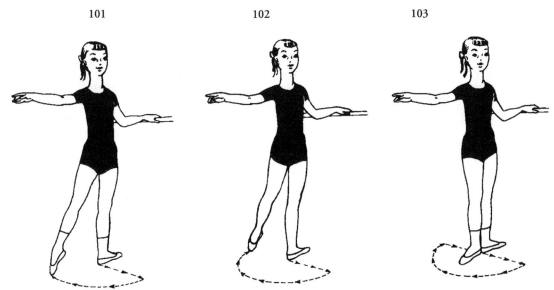

101   102   103

Ronds de Jambe à Terre, en Dedans

(rawn deh zhamb ah tair, ahn deh-dahn')

You do this exactly as I have described the outward circles of the leg, but reverse the movement of the foot. After the *port de bras* preparation point the right foot to Fourth Position back on count "One," then slide the toes around to Second Position on count "two," slide the toes to Fourth Position front on "three," and return the foot to perfect First Position on "four."

Do this exercise eight times with each foot.

Port de Bras au Corps Cambré

(por deh brah oh cor cahm-bray')

104   105   106   107   108

This is an important exercise to practice because it will stretch the muscles and ligaments of your back and thighs and knees. At the same time it will help you to acquire graceful movements of the arms and head.

104. Ready. Stand in Fifth Position (you may stand in First Position for the first few months) with the right foot front and the left hand on the barre.

105. Bend forward from the hips. Keep your ribs well lifted up even though you are bending forward. Do not allow your knees to bend, but as you stretch forward pull your knees up tighter. Be careful to stay forward over the balls of the feet and not to pull back into the heels. Reach for the floor with your right hand. Count slowly and bend slowly. Count "And one, and two…"

106. Straighten up. The right arm is stretched forward in front of your chest. Count "And three…"

107. Raise the right arm up higher so that it is over your head. Be careful not to allow the right shoulder to hunch up. Look up toward your hand. Count "And four…"

109 110

108. Bend straight back from the hips. As you do so, push your seat forward and keep pulling up tightly on the knees. Allow the head to drop back. Count "And five, and six…"

109. Open the right arm out to Second Position and turn your head to the right so that you are looking at your hand. Count "And seven…"

110. Straighten up. Count "And eight."

Repeat this exercise four times on each side.

DON'T DO THIS!

111. Don't pull back into the heels as you bend forward.

111

DON'T DO THIS!

112. Don't bend back from the waist, letting the seat stick out in back.

112

Battements Frappés

(baht-mahn' frah-pay')

113

This is another very important exercise for you to practice carefully and slowly. It will develop great strength in the insteps of your feet and in your thighs. Another reason why it is important for you to learn this step correctly is that it forms part of the jumping step called *jeté*.

Stand in Fifth Position with the right foot front and the left hand on the barre. As you do your *port de bras* preparation raise your right foot to a flexed position on your left ankle.

113. Ready. Your right heel is crossed in front of your left ankle bone. The foot is not pointed but flexed; that is, it forms a right angle to your leg. Don't allow the toes to stick up or to curl down, keep them softly pressed downward. Remember to stand up tall out of your hips and do not sit in the left hip. Keep the weight forward over the ball of the left foot, press the right knee out and back. Try to open from the hip as much as possible.

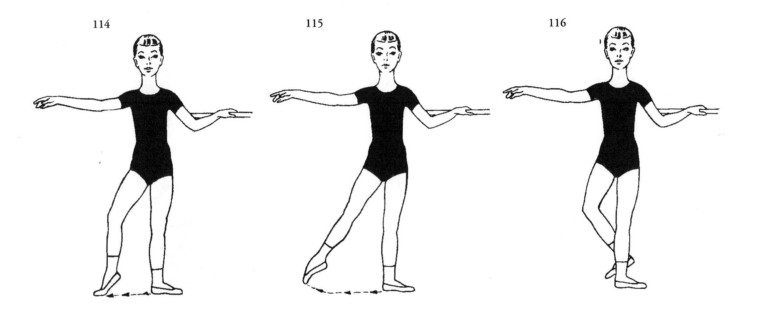

114   115   116

114. Brush the right foot downward and outward so that the ball of the foot strikes the floor. Count "And…"

115. Point the right foot hard and at the same time snap the right knee straight. Allow the toes to be about three inches of the floor. Count "One…"

116. Bend the right knee and bring the right foot to rest in back of the left ankle. Cross the right heel to the anklebone. Count "And two."

Practice this exercise slowly sixteen times with each foot. Alternate, crossing in front and in back of the supporting ankle. Use strength in thrusting the foot out. This is not a weak movement. Be sure to strike the ball of the foot on the floor each time. The only movement of the exercise takes place in the knee and ankle joints. NEVER raise or lower your thigh.

Battements Retirés

(baht-mahn' reh-teer-ay')

117

This exercise is a basic movement of ballet technique and will strengthen you for *adagio* (slow and controlled movements and extensions of the legs). Practice it with great care so that you work correctly through your hips. Do not allow the hip to raise up when the knee lifts, but press the hip down so that both hips remain straight and even. At the same time lift yourself tall out of both hips.

Stand in First Position with the left hand on the barre. Prepare with a *port de bras* as in 67 through 70.

117. Ready. Check your posture and placement. Your seat must be well under and the stomach well lifted.

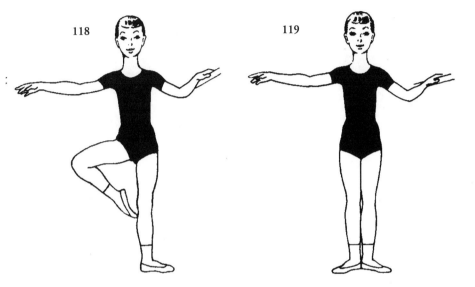

118

119

119. Return the right foot to First Position on count "And three…" Hold First Position on "And four."

Repeat the exercise eight times with each foot.

120. Don't do this!

120

118. Draw the right foot up the side of the left leg until the toes of the right foot touch the little hollow at the side of the left knee. Keep the right foot well pointed so the heel is far away from the left leg. Open the right knee as far back as possible. Remember not to let your hip go up, press the right hip down so it stays even with the left hip.

Hold your weight forward over the ball of your left foot; don't pull back into the left heel. Be very careful that your right foot is pointing straight—press the heel front and the toes back so that the foot does not "sickle" (point crookedly). Count "And one…" as the foot raises up. Hold the position on "And two…"

Grands Battements

(grahn baht-mahn')

The grands battements will make you more limber so that you can move your legs more freely. It will make the muscles of your back and stomach very strong, too, if you work to control each movement and remember to hold yourself properly as you work.

Although the drawings show this exercise from Fifth Position, you should practice it from First Position for the first few months until you are able to do good *battements tendus* from Fifth Position, because the *battement tendu* is the basis of this exercise. The drawings have purposely been made without extreme turn-out. This is to remind you not to turn your feet out more than you are able to do with the entire leg from the hip joint.

For the beginner to achieve straight knees and good posture, it is wise to practice this exercise in four counts. Later, when you have been dancing for about a year, you will take the leg up and down without the pauses.

GRANDS BATTEMENTS À LA QUATRIÈME DEVANT

Stand in First Position or Fifth Position with the right foot front, left hand on the barre. Prepare with a *port de bras* as in 67 through 70.

121

122

121. Ready. Check for posture and placement.

122. Slide the right foot front to point in Fourth Position, as in *battement tendu*. Count "One..."

123. Raise the right leg up as high as you can while keeping both hips in line and even. You will have to pull the right hip back a little because if it goes forward when the leg raises, your leg will be turned in. Stretch your right leg so the knee is very straight. Pull the supporting knee up tight. Lift up your stomach and your ribs so that you are very tall. Try to raise the leg as high as your hips, but do not bend forward or back to get it up. Keep both shoulders straight and low. Count "Two…"

124. Lower the right toes to the floor in Fourth Position; don't put any weight on them. Count "Three…"

125. Slide the right foot back to First Position or Fifth Position in front of the left foot. "And four." Be sure not to bend the right knee.

126. DON'T DO THIS!

GRANDS BATTEMENTS À LA SECONDE

This is a most difficult exercise. It is especially hard to keep your correct placement in this exercise, but you must try very hard to do so or the exercise has no value for you.

If you remember not to throw your weight onto the working foot, it will help you. All the weight must remain over the ball of the supporting foot at all times and the working leg must go up and down without any help from any other part of the body. Keep your shoulders facing straight front, very relaxed, and pressed down low in the back. Don't let them hunch up when you raise your leg. Keep both of your hips facing straight front and even. Don't twist outward from the barre. Your spine must be very straight all through the exercise.

Hold your head erect and look straight ahead. I hope you have not forgotten to do this on all the exercises as you practiced; your head is a very important part of your body and your eyes play a big part in your balance.

Stand in First Position or in Fifth Position with the right foot in front of the left foot. Prepare with a *port de bras*.

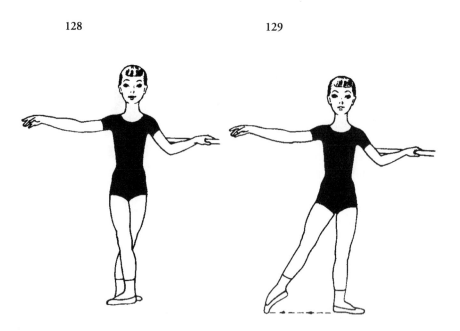

128   129

128. Ready. Check for posture and placement.

129. Slide the right foot out to point in Second Position as in *battement tendu*. Count "One…"

130. Raise the right leg. Be careful not to lean to the right or the left or to move in your shoulders. Press the right hip down, as the leg comes up, so that it stays even with the left hip. Keep both knees pulled up tight and straight. Press your seat under and hold the heel forward. Count "Two…"

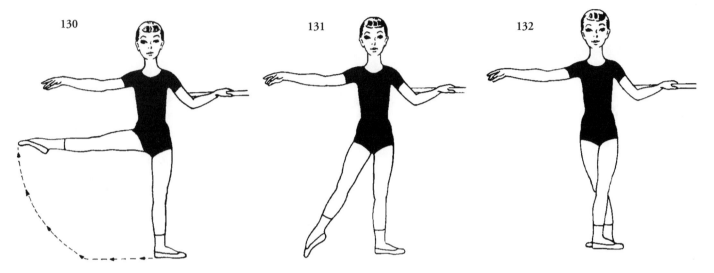

131. Lower the toes to the floor in Second Position. Don't put any weight on them. Count "Three..."

132. Slide the right foot into First Position or Fifth Position in back of the left foot. Count "Four." Don't allow the knees to bend to come into position.

Do this exercise eight times with each leg. If you are practicing it from Fifth Position, close the right foot alternately in back and in front of the left foot.

133. 134. DON'T DO THIS!

GRANDS BATTEMENTS À LA QUATRIÈME DERRIÈRE

Practice this exercise facing the barre. Center your weight over the ball of the supporting foot and do not rock back and forth as your leg moves up and down. Hold your shoulders at their normal position; do not press them back. Hold your ribs up, but don't sway your back. Keep your head erect; do not look down.

135   136

135. Ready. Both hands holding the barre lightly. Check for posture and placement. Stand in First Position or in Fifth Position with the right foot in back of the left foot.

136. Slide the right foot back to point in Fourth Position. Keep your weight forward over the ball of the left foot. Both shoulders straight front. Count "One…"

50

137   138   139

137. Raise the right leg up. Do not allow the weight to fall back into the left heel, press forward. Keep both knees pulled up tight and straight. Don't press your shoulders back; hold them naturally and be sure that the right shoulder is in line with the left shoulder. Don't drop your head; look straight ahead. Count "Two…"

138. Lower the toes to the floor. Do not put any weight on them. Count "Three…"

139. Slide the right foot into First Position or Fifth Position in back of the left foot. Count "Four."

Repeat this exercise eight times with each foot.

Battements Soutenus, à la Seconde

(baht-mahn' soo-ten-oo')

T his exercise is especially valuable to improve the step called *assemblé*, which is one of the basic *allegro* steps of ballet. As you practice it, be very conscious of the position of your hips so that you do not sit in the hip over the supporting leg or allow the hip on the side of the working leg to push out of line. Be perfectly *centered*. Watch carefully that you do not roll inward on the arch of your foot as you *plié*; keep the knee directly over the toes and the spine very straight.

Stand in Fifth Position (or in First if you are not yet ready for Fifth) with the right foot in front of the left. Prepare with a *port de bras* as in 67 through 70.

140

140. Ready. Check for posture and placement.

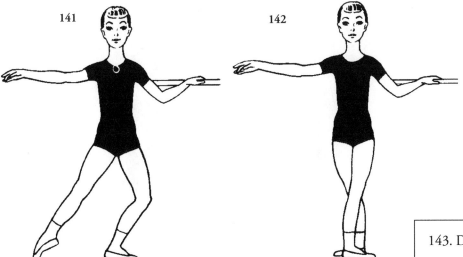

141

142

143. DON'T DO THIS!

143

141. Slide the right foot out to point in Second Position and as it slides out allow the left knee to bend in a good *demi-plié*. Keep your head erect; don't turn your shoulders away from front. Count "And one…"

142. Slide the right foot into Fifth Position (or First Position) in back of the left foot and at the same time straighten the left knee so that both knees are pulled up tight and straight as you finish. Count "And two."

Practice this exercise sixteen times with each foot. If you are working from Fifth Position, close the right foot alternately in back and in front of the left foot.

Relevés

(reh-leh-vay')

144. In First Position: Ready. Face the barre. Hold it lightly with both hands. Check yourself for perfect posture and placement. Keep the head erect and look straight forward. Turn your legs outward only as far as you can without straining to keep from rolling in on the arches. Pull the knees up tight.

145. Rise on the balls of the feet pulling the heels straight up through the ankle, knees still very straight. Press the balls of the feet into the floor and feel all of your toes on the floor. Count "And one, and two…"

146. Lower the heels gently and very slowly to the floor, pulling the knees up tightly as you do so. Count "And three, and four." Take the whole two counts to lower the heels.

Practice these *relevés* in First Position eight times, and then do the same thing in Second Position eight times.

147 148 149

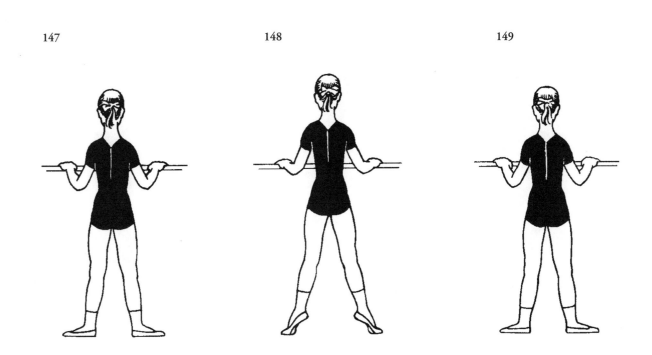

147. Ready.

148. "And one, and two…"

149. "And three, and four."

These *relevés* are meant to develop strength in your feet, ankles, and legs. They will help you to jump better in allegro steps and will prepare you for dancing *sur les pointes* (on the toes). Practice them slowly and with great care for posture and placement.

II
Basic Center Exercises

Note To Students

The old adage says, "Practice makes perfect," and this is especially true about ballet technique. We ballet dancers have not only to perfect our technique, we also have to construct the instrument with which we perform this technique. The musician plays an instrument already constructed for him, the artist paints on a canvas, but the dancer must shape and form his own body into the instrument of his art. That is one reason why it takes many years to develop a good ballet dancer.

The exercises we practice at the barre shape and strengthen the legs, feet, and back, making them capable of performing the difficult technical feats required of them. If you have been faithfully attending your ballet classes and practicing your barre exercises, you are slowly but surely building strength in your feet and legs, stretching your tendons and muscles, improving your turn-out, and acquiring elasticity in your knees.

In order to be a successful and accomplished ballet dancer, you must have good "line," or a sense of the design your body makes in space. Your poses and movement must have grace and elegance. There must be style and quality in your dancing. All of these things you acquire under the guidance of a good teacher, but there must be on your part a tremendous drive and desire to strive for perfection in every detail of technique and artistry. You must be willing and eager to work hard to develop your body physically and to achieve with it the successful execution of the difficult steps and movements of ballet.

Study the drawings in this section carefully and understand the body line before you attempt to perform them with your own body. Fix in your mind the correct way to hold your hand, head or arm, the position of the shoulders, the line of the leg in relation to the back and the arm. Spend a good part of your practice time working to improve your *port de bras,* to get the feel of the *arabesques, attitudes,* and body positions. Stand in front of your mirror and check your movements carefully against the drawings in this book. When you see good results in the mirror, turn around and try to do the same thing without seeing yourself. A dancer must learn to *feel* poses and movements and not depend on seeing the mirrored reflection.

Port de Bras

(por deh brah): Carriage of the arms

If you have the best legs and feet in the world and do not have a good *port de bras*, you will not be successful as a dancer.

Your individuality as a dancer, your grace, your beauty of form and line, your sense of style and movement—all of these things show in the way you hold your head and arms and in the way you move them.

It is not easy to develop a good *port de bras*. It will take many hours, weeks, months, and years of conscious effort on your part and on the part of your teacher—for stylized, graceful, flowing movements of the arms are even more difficult to achieve than skill with the feet and legs. You must spend much time practicing intelligently, trying to constantly improve the positions and movements of your hands, arms, and head.

Look carefully at the drawings that follow. In your arms and hands try to feel the lift of the elbows, the roundness of the line, the firmness without tension of the wrists, the grouping of the fingers. Your arms should feel light. If they feel heavy, it is probably because they are too tense. There must be no strain in your arms, hands, neck or shoulders when you do *port de bras*. The arms move slowly when passing from one position to another, flowing in perfect harmony with the musical phrasing of a lovely lyrical waltz.

1   2

THE HAND AND THE ARM IN BALLET

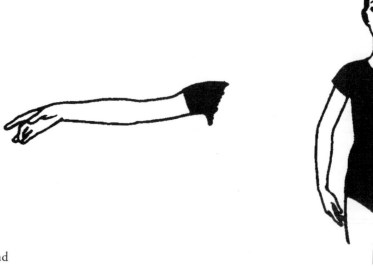

1. The grouping of the fingers: the hand must look round, but long and slender as well, if it is to appear graceful. There must be no angles in the hand. The thumb is held under and the index finger is slightly separated from the others with the third finger slightly indented. The fingers are spaced very slightly apart and held round but not bent.

2. Position of the hand and arm when held downward: the grouping of the fingers remains the same no matter whether the hand is held down, up, or out to the side. Notice the wrist. It must be held firm but not stiff or tense, round but not bent or *broken* in its line. The elbow, too, must be round, not bent and not straight.

62

3-4. Position of the hand and arm when held in front: keep the elbow high and round. When both arms are extended in front of you, imagine that you are using them to encircle a large, oval-shaped beach ball. Then you will get the feeling of holding the elbows up properly. The palms of the hand face toward the body and there is a slight downward slope from the wrists.

5. Position of the hand and arm when held upward: once again be careful not to *break* at the wrist. Palms face in; do not turn the palm to the audience. Be careful to hold the elbow round but not bent, stretched but not stiff.

6

7

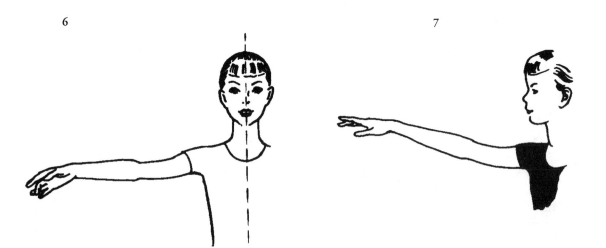

6. Position of the hand and arm when held out to the side: this position is the most difficult one for beginners. It is not easy to keep the elbow up in the correct position, as it seems more natural, at first, to allow the elbow to drop. Later the correct position becomes natural as you form the habit of constantly feeling the lift in the elbow. Do not allow the hand to droop at the wrist or to curl inward. Once again, the hand is an extension of the arm, with the wrist held firm. Try not to open your hand so that you look like a traffic policeman giving a signal, but maintain the fingers in their correct grouping with the hand neither completely open nor completely turned palm downward. The correct position lies between these two extremes

7. The hand in arabesque position: the grouping of the fingers remains the same, but now the palm faces downward toward the floor. Hold the wrist firm, and do not allow the hand to droop from the wrist. Stretch the fingers out completely, with a feeling of life in them, and do not let them feel relaxed or dead.

9

9. Don't let your fingers get stiff or tense, because this is most ungraceful in movement. Keep the thumb under, not "sticking out like a sore thumb."

10

8

8. Incorrect positions of the hand: don't let your fingers curl like the claws of a little dead bird. This gives your hand a stubby and dull appearance.

10. Don't let your wrist break, or your elbow drop. These are both very bad faults.

Basic Arm Positions

There are three distinct schools of ballet technique – the French, the Italian, and the Russian. In *port de bras* each school of technique has a different set of numbers for the basic positions of the arms. This is because in the French school there are six basic arm positions, in the Italian school there are eight basic arm positions, and in the Russian school there are four basic arm positions.

The form of these positions is practically the same in all the schools even though they may be called by different numbers. In other words, a correct position is equally correct in all schools. In this book I am giving you a set of numbered basic positions, based on the fundamental positions of all three, as taught at my own school. These positions correspond to the five positions of the feet although there are more than five basic arm positions.

Do not be disturbed if your teacher calls any of these positions by a number different from one given in this book, but strive for perfection of the position according to the drawing.

11. First Position (arms in repose according to the French school): The finger tips barely touch the thighs. The elbows are round and held away from the body. Check yourself for all points discussed in 2. This basic position is often used when doing *allegro*, or jumping, steps and in *chaîné* turns.

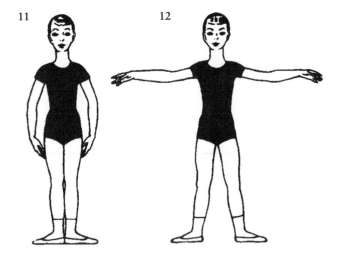

12. Second Position (same in all three schools): The arms extend in a curved line from finger tip to finger tip just slightly below shoulder level and slightly forward. Do not press them too far back so that your shoulders are forced out of line, but hold them slightly forward so that your shoulders remain normal. Check yourself for all points given in 6. Take care that the arms are not held higher than the shoulders or dropped too low, and be sure to keep both at the same level. This position of the arms is used very often in dancing and is most difficult to do gracefully, so practice it often.

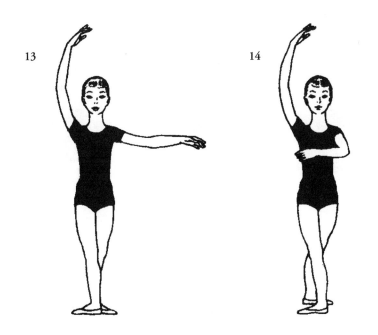

13. Third Position (Fourth Position en haut of the Cecchetti, or Italian, school): this may be done with either the right or the left arm raised. Practice both, of course. When you raise your arm, be sure that you do not raise the shoulder with it. Press the shoulders down firmly so that they look relaxed and your neck looks long and graceful. Check your elbows, wrists, and hands according to 5 and 6. This is the attitude position of the arms and is used in many of the body positions (see 101 through 124, and 137 through 141). It is also used in allegro steps such as the assemblé.

14. Fourth Position High (Fourth Position of the French school): there are two Fourth Positions of the arms. Here again, the raised arm may be either the right or the left. Check 3, 4, and 5 for corrections. The low arm crosses the body in front of the ribs, palm facing in toward the body, the hand in front of the opposite breast. This position of the arms is sometimes used in such allegro steps as pas de chat.

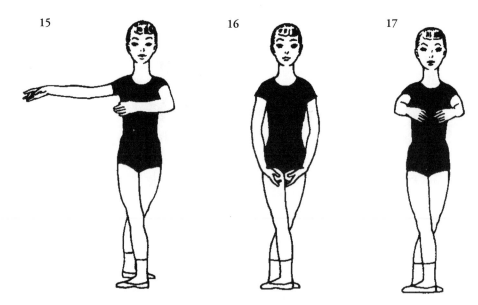

15   16   17

15. Fourth Position Front (Similar to the Fourth Position en avant of the Cecchetti school): this position may be taken with either the right or the left arm held in front of the body. The front arm crosses the body palm facing in, the hand in front of the opposite breast. Keep the elbow lifted. Other arm is extended to Second Position. Check yourself carefully for all points discussed in 4 and 6. This position of the arms is used as a preparation for pirouettes, and for such allegro steps as glissade, pas de chat, brisé, and jeté.

16. Fifth Position Low (Preparatory Position according to the Russian and French schools): there are three Fifth positions of the arms. Whenever the arms form a circle, we are in Fifth Position—low, front or high. Check 2 for corrections in practicing this position. The hands should be several inches apart. This position of the arms is used in allegro steps such as changement de pied and glissade, in the pirouette, and in transition from one pose to another.

17. Fifth Position Front (First Position according to the Russian and French schools): this is a transitional position used when passing the arms from one position to another. Arms are held in front of the ribs, hands several inches apart. Check 3 for corrections.

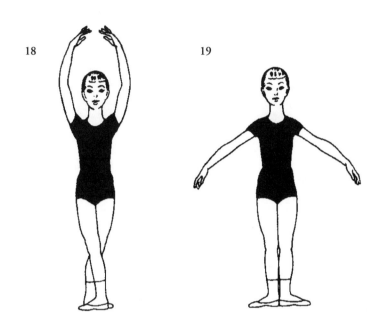

18. Fifth Position High (Third Position according to the Russian school): the arms reach upward as far as possible without raising the shoulders. They should make a frame for the head; therefore, they are held slightly forward. Elbows should be round but not bent. Fingertips are several inches apart as in all Fifth Positions. Check 5 for corrections. This position is very often used in dancing.

19. *Demi-seconde* Position (deh'-mee seh-cohnd', Half Second Position): while this is not one of the "five positions" that correspond to the five positions of the feet, it is nevertheless a basic position because it is used very often in dancing particularly in allegro, or jumping, movements. The arms are held in position between First and Second, slightly forward. Elbows are round, palms face each other, and wrists are held firm.

In practicing these basic positions, and the movements of the *port de bras* later, remember to try to keep the arms light and weightless. If they are tense and stiff the appearance will be strained and the arms will tire quickly. It is impossible to move them gracefully under such conditions.

The Head in Ballet

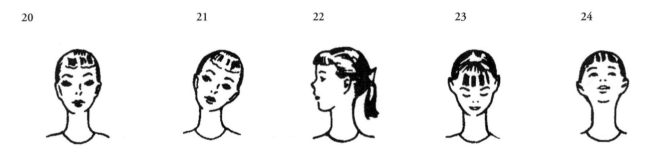

20   21   22   23   24

You must train your head to move gracefully and you must discipline it in training just as you do your feet, legs, and arms. If you do not learn to do this, your dancing will appear wooden, colorless, lifeless, and dull. Right from the beginning at the barre you have been practicing to hold your head erect and not to let it loll around. Now you must learn to incline the head, to turn it, to lower it, and to raise it at will and in harmony with the movements of the other parts of your body. You must give a great deal of thought to the movements of the head, because if you do not think about it as you dance you will either hold it stiffly in one place or it will wobble around while your gaze shifts from place to place. Keep your eyes open and lively. Don't develop a fixed stare into space or up to the ceiling.

20. The head erect.
21. The head inclined: this is a slightly tilted position of the head. It is most important in conjunction with the epaulement,–the use of the shoulders in ballet (see page 25). It is used in the various poses of the body to give grace and movement to the pose.
22. The head turned: in dancing we often turn the head to one side or the other. When you do this, keep your eyes open and really look in the direction to which you turn your head.
23. The head lowered.
24. The head raised.

Port de Bras Exercise 1

Here is a basic port de bras exercise for you to practice. Most likely your teacher gives this exercise in class. Check yourself during practice sessions for corrections on all the positions used in this exercise.

Music for the *port de bras* exercise generally is a waltz. Each count given here corresponds to one measure of waltz time. In moving the arms from one position to another move them slowly and steadily, filling out the musical phrase. Be careful not to move them mechanically or jerkily. Repeat these four counts or measures eight times on each side.

25

25. Ready to begin: stand in Fifth Position with the right foot front. Face the lower left corner of the room. Stand in as good a Fifth Position as you are able to do without rolling in on your arches. If you cannot take Fifth Position comfortably, stand in Third Position. Always remember that the turn-out of the legs begins at the hips and that it is the turn-out of the thighs that controls the turn-out of the feet. Hold the Fifth or Third Position of the feet firmly throughout the exercise and keep the thigh muscles pulled up tightly so that both knees are straight. Check yourself for correct body placement so that you have good posture. This is essential, for if you do not stand properly you will not appear graceful in your movements. Incline your head to the left and hold the arms in Fifth Position Low.

26   27   28   29

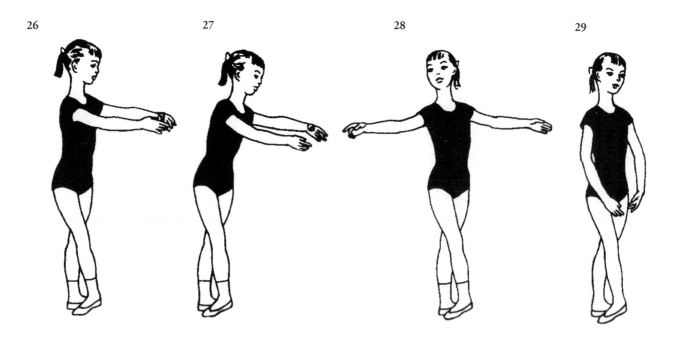

26. Count "And one…" Raise both arms to Fifth Position Front with a very slight forward movement of your upper body. The head is still inclined to the left. Look into the palms of the hands.

27. Count "And two…" Open the hands outward from the wrists.

28. Count "And three…" Open both arms outward to Second Position. Allow the head to follow the movement of the right arm so that it turns to the right simultane-ously with the movement of the arms. The movement of the arms takes place from the shoulders, not from the elbows.

29. Count "And four…" Gently turn the hands over so that the palms face downward. Lower both arms slowly to Fifth Position Low. As the arms are lowered, follow the movement of the right hand with your eyes and allow your head to turn naturally to the starting position (inclined to the left shoulder).

Port de Bras Exercise 2

30

Here is another basic port de bras. Practice the basic arm positions carefully until you feel sure of them before working on these *port de bras* exercises. The counts are the same as in the preceding exercise.

30. Ready to begin: stand in Fifth Position with the right foot front. Face the lower left corner of the room. Head is inclined to the left and the arms are in Fifth Position Low.

31.   32.   33.   34.   35.

31. Count "And…" Raise both arms to Fifth Position Front.

32. Count "One…" Continue the upward movement of the arms, raising the arms to Fifth Position High. You are still facing the corner of the room. Raise your head a little as you raise your arms, and look up toward your hands.

33. Count "And two…" Turn the upper body to face the front of the room. Keep the arms in Fifth Position High and turn the head with the body.

34. Count "And three…" Open both arms to Second Position. Turn the head to follow the right hand as it is lowered.

35. Count "And four…" Turn the hands over so that the palms face downward, and lower both arms slowly to Fifth Position Low. At the same time follow the movement of the right hand with the eyes so that the head slowly returns to its starting position.

Practice these four measures or counts eight times on each side. Keep the arms light, the hands alive; don't tense. Try to move the arms freely and simply. Always remember that simplicity is the greatest thing in art. Simple movements of the hands and arms enhance grace.

74

Center Barre Exercises

It is most important to practice away from the barre the same exercises we learn holding the barre. But now, in doing these exercises in the center, we add the use of the shoulders and head to the movements of the feet and legs. This is called "épaulement."

THE ÉPAULEMENT
(ay-pol-mahn'): The use of the shoulders

The use of the shoulders and head in ballet are what gives life, style, and form to your movements. *Épaulement* is not easy to learn and requires much concentration and practice. You must work at it consistently and with real thought until you find that it becomes second nature to you and you can fall into correct positions naturally without having to pause to think about them.

36. Head and shoulders in alignment with the leg. When the right leg is pointed to Second Position, the right shoulder is brought slightly forward and the head is turned a little to the right and inclined to the right shoulder. Be very careful not to exaggerate the tilt of the head. This épaulement in alignment with the leg is generally used when traveling from the back to the front.

37. Head and shoulders in opposition to the leg. When the right leg is pointed to Second Position, the left shoulder is brought slightly forward and the head is turned a

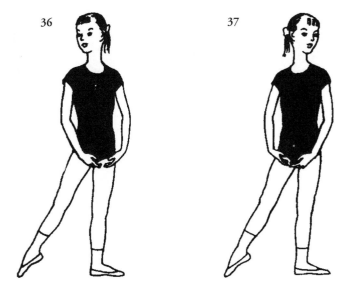

little to the left and inclined to the left shoulder. The épaulement in opposition is generally used in traveling from the front to the back.

As you progress in your study of ballet, you will grow in strength and your balance will improve. Eventually you will be able to do in the center all of the exercises you take at the barre; but, for now, practice only the *battements tendus, battements soutenus,* and the *grands battements.*

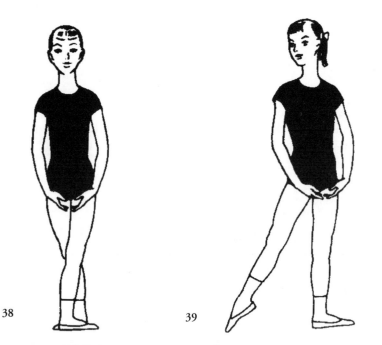

38

39

BATTEMENTS TENDUS, ADVANCING
(baht-mahn' tahn-doo')

This exercise is done with *épaulement* in alignment.

38. Ready to begin. Stand in Fifth Position with the right foot behind. Take care that you are correctly placed, have your head erect, your eyes lively and looking straight out, not up.

39. Count "One..." Slide the right foot out to a strong point in Second Position. At the same time turn the upper body slightly so that the right shoulder is brought a little more forward than the left, and look toward the lower right corner of the room, inclining the head slightly toward the right shoulder. Position of the shoulders and head is *écarté* (see 114). Take care not to allow the right leg or foot to turn in.

40   41   42

40. Count "Two…" Slide the right foot into Fifth Position in front of the left foot. At the same time turn the upper body, and the head, to face straight front. Keep both knees straight.

41. Count "Three…" Slide the left foot out to a strong point in Second Position. At the same time turn the upper body slightly so that the left shoulder is brought a little more forward than the right, and look toward the lower left corner of the room, inclining the head slightly toward the left shoulder. Position of the shoulders and head is *écarté*. Take care not to allow the left leg or foot to turn in.

42. Count "Four…" Slide the left foot into Fifth Position in front of the right foot. At the same time turn the upper body and the head to face straight front. Keep both knees straight.

Repeat this exercise sixteen times in all, traveling forward and alternating the feet and the turn of the shoulders.

43   44   45

BATTEMENTS TENDUS, RETREATING

This exercise is done with *épaulement* in opposition.

43. Ready to begin: stand in Fifth Position with the right foot behind.

44. Count "One…" Slide the left foot out to a strong point in Second Position. At the same time turn the upper body slightly so that the right shoulder is brought slightly more forward than the left, and look toward the lower right corner of the room, inclining the head slightly to the right. Position of the shoulders and head is *éffacé*.

45. Count "Two…" Slide the left foot into Fifth Position in back of the right foot. At the same time turn the upper body and the head straight front. Keep both knees straight.

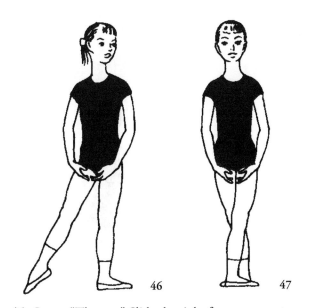

Repeat this exercise sixteen times in all, traveling back and alternating the feet and the turn of the shoulders. You may also practice traveling forward eight times and back eight times without pausing between.

This exercise should also be practiced with a demi-plié in Fifth Position each time the foot is closed in.

Be very careful to maintain the turn-out of the pointed leg.

46. Count "Three..." Slide the right foot out to a strong point in Second Position. At the same time turn the upper body slightly so that the *left* shoulder is brought slightly more forward than the right, and look toward the lower left corner of the room, inclining the head slightly to the left. Position of the shoulders and head is *éffacé* (see 118).

47. Count "Four..." Slide the right foot into Fifth Position in back of the left foot. At the same time turn the upper body and the head straight front. Keep both knees straight.

48. DON'T DO THIS!

SIMPLE BATTEMENTS SOUTENUS

(baht-mahn' soo-ten-oo')

This exercise is most valuable to prepare you for *assemblés* and *jetés*, which are basic *allegro*, or jumping, steps of ballet. The exercise is done just as you have been practicing it at the barre.

It is illustrated here, without the *épaulement*, in its most simple form. When your teacher tells you that you are doing it properly, you may try to practice it with the *épaulement* just as it is described for the *battement tendus*.

Stand in Fifth Position with the right foot back and the arms in Fifth Position Low. Take two counts to prepare with the arms. On count "One" raise both arms to Fifth Position Front. On count "Two" open both arms to Second Position.

49

50

49. Ready to begin.

50. Count, "One…" Slide the right foot out to a strong point in Second Position. At the same time bend the left knee in a *demi-plié*. Take care not to roll in on the arch of the left foot, keep the right leg well turned out at the thigh so that the knee faces up to the ceiling. Do not allow the pointed foot to twist so that the toes are out of line with the heel. Keep the hips in alignment and the body well lifted up out of the hips. Keep the ribs lifted and the shoulders pressed down low.

51   52   53

51. Count "Two…" Slide the right foot into Fifth Position in front of the left foot. At the same time straighten the left knee, pulling both knees up tightly.

52. Count "Three…" Repeat the movement of count "One" with the left leg sliding out. Hold the head erect.

53. Count "Four…" Slide the left foot into Fifth Position in front of the right foot, straightening both knees.

Repeat these four counts until you have done the exercise sixteen times, alternating right and left leg. Practice it the same way reversing the action and traveling from front to back.

54. Don't sit into the supporting hip.

54   55

55. Don't allow the hip on the side of the working leg to raise.

GRANDS BATTEMENTS
(grahn baht-mahn')

This is an important exercise to practice away from the barre; it helps you to achieve a sense of balance through the body. In order to take the leg up and down, without wobbling, it is necessary to be well centered and placed, and to maintain control through the hips.

GRANDS BATTEMENTS *à la quatrième devant* (ah lah caht-ree-em' deh-vahn'): we are going to practice our *grands battements en croix* (ahn crwah), which means "in the form of a cross." This begins with the grands battements taken directly forward to Fourth Position. Of course we have been practicing our *battements* at the barre, but now we do the same exercise without the aid of the barre and we use our arms and head in harmony, and in coordination with the movements of the leg and foot.

56. Ready to begin. Stand in Fifth Position with the right foot front. Face directly front with the head erect and the arms in Fifth Position Low. Take a two-count preparation with the arms.

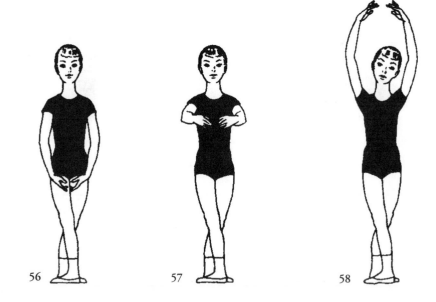

57. Count "One…" Raise the arms to Fifth Position Front.

58. Count "Two…" Raise the arms to Fifth Position High. Incline the head slightly to the left, chin slightly up, eyes looking straight out. The exercise begins. Each *grand battement* is counted in four.

59. Slide the right foot front to a strong point in Fourth Position. Count "One…" (pictured on next page)

60. Raise the right leg to hip level. Keep both hips in alignment. The right hip must be pulled back a little as the leg is raised so that the thigh remains

59 60 61 62 63

turned out. Keep both knees pulled up tightly. Lift stomach and ribs. Do not bend forward or backward. Press both shoulders down low. Count "Two…"

61. Lower the right foot to point on the floor again in Fourth Position. Do not allow your weight to fall forward onto the pointing foot, but keep it well balanced over the ball of the supporting foot. Keep well lifted up out of the hips. Count "Three…"

62. Slide the right foot into Fifth Position in front of the left foot. Count "Four…" Repeat these four counts, doing the exercise four times in all.

63. On the fourth count of the fourth time you do this exercise lower both arms from Fifth Position High to Fifth Position Front. Straighten the head.

64. Don't do this!

64

GRANDS BATTEMENTS *à la seconde* (grahn baht-mahn' ah lah seh-cohnd'): Raising the leg in Second Position is the most difficult to master correctly. Make every effort to hold the body in its correct placement. If you are careless about this as you work in class and in practicing, you will form bad habits that will later prevent you from mastering the more difficult steps and movements of ballet technique. In this way you will defeat yourself.

65. Ready to begin. As this is a continuation of the *grands battements* taken to Fourth Position in front, we begin from the last position at the end of the fourth *grand battement.*

66. Slide the right foot out to a strong point in Second Position. At the same time open both arms out to Second Position. Hold the head erect, and look straight forward. Count "One..."

67. Raise the right leg to hip height. If you are not able to take the leg to this height and still keep your

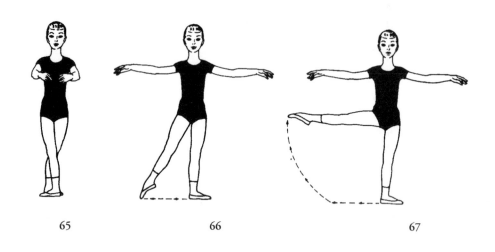

65   66   67

body centered and your hips in line, raise the leg only as high as you can safely take it. The height of your extension is not important to you at this stage of your development. The leg will go up high easily after you gain strength and improved placement. Remember not to move your shoulders or lean to the right or left. Keep the right hip pressed down so that both hips are in line. Both knees must be pulled up tight. Hold your seat under and the right leg well turned out from the hip. Don't lose the lift out of the hips! Count "Two..."

68

69

70

68. Lower the right foot to point on the floor. Remember not to shift your weight from the supporting foot to the pointing foot. Count "Three..."

69. Slide the right foot into Fifth Position in front of the left foot. Don't let the knee bend as it comes into position. Count "Four..."

Repeat these four counts four times. Alternate closing the right foot in front of the left foot and in back of it so that the second and fourth times your right foot is in back of your left. Hold the arms in a good Second Position throughout the exercise.

70. On the fourth count of the fourth time you do this exercise lower both arms to Fifth Position Low. Head is still erect.

GRANDS BATTEMENTS *à la quatrième derrière* (grahn baht-mahn' ah lah caht-ree-em' dair-ee-air'): remember to take your weight forward over the ball of the supporting foot throughout this exercise, and do not rock your body back and forth as your leg moves up and down. The leg must be taken directly back in line with the heel of the supporting foot; do not allow it to go to the side.

71. Ready to begin. As this is a continuation of the *grands battements* to Fourth Position Front and to Second Position, we start in the position in which we finished our *battements à la seconde.*

72. Slide the right foot directly back to a strong point in Fourth Position. At the same time raise both arms to Fifth Position Front and incline the head slightly to the right. Remember to point on the inside of the big toe and to keep the heel pressed down and forward. Do not let your right shoulder pull back toward the leg but keep it in line with the left shoulder. Count "One..."

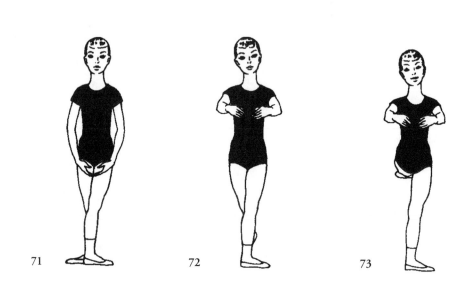

71   72   73

73. Raise the right leg up to hip height. The weight of the body must not fall back into the left heel, but is pressed forward. Pull the knees up very tightly. It is especially hard to keep the one in the air straight, in this position, so concentrate on it. Count "Two..."

86

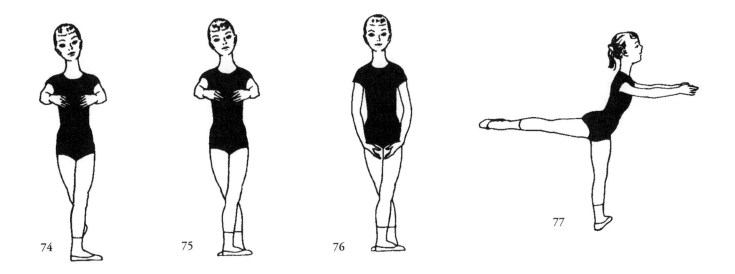

74

75

76

77

74. Lower the right foot to a point again on the floor. Do not transfer your weight so that you fall back to the pointed foot. Count "Three…"

75. Slide the right foot into Fifth Position in back of the left foot. Hold the arms in Fifth Position Front and keep the head inclined to the right throughout the exercise. Count "Four…"

Repeat these four counts four times. Now repeat the *grands battements à la seconde* exactly as described in figures 65–70. The only difference is that you take the right foot in back of the left foot the first time so that the right foot finishes in front of the left foot on the last *grand battement* exactly as you began the entire exercise in figures 56–63.

76. End of *grands battements* exercise.

77. Side view of grands battements to Fourth Position in the back.

Repeat the entire exercise with the left foot.

Adagio
(ah-dah'-zhee-oh)

Adagio is an Italian word meaning "at leisure." In music *adagio* movements are slow, leisurely, sustained passages. In ballet *adagio* is a succession of slow and graceful movements consisting of *pliés, ports de bras, développés,* turns, and poses that may be very simple and that become more complex in advanced stages of development. These exercises develop strength, power, balance, and line, to give your dancing grace and nobility. Here is a very simple *adagio* for you to practice carefully and with much thought. It consists of a *grand plié* followed by a *port de bras* and three *développés.* Body placement is of the utmost importance in *adagio.* Work carefully to be centered and lifted, and to keep the hips and shoulders in alignment.

GRAND PLIÉ IN FIFTH POSITION

78. Ready to begin. Face *en croisé* (ahn crwah-zay'), that is, face the lower left corner, standing in Fifth Position with the right foot front. Arms are in Fifth Position Low, head is inclined to the left. Move to slow counts.

78

88

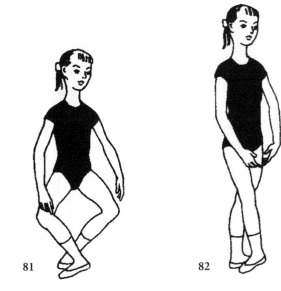

79

80

81

82

79. *Demi-plié* in Fifth Position. Open the knees well, and keep the heels and all five toes firmly on the floor. Hold the back strong by lifting up out of the hips. Count "And one..."

80. Continue the *plié*, allowing the heels to raise up slightly. Hold the ankles firm, don't let the heels slip forward, press all the toes into the floor. Keep lifting up as the knees bend lower. Count "And two..."

81. As soon as you touch bottom, start to come up. When you are halfway up, lower both heels so that you are again in the *demi-plié* position. Keep your seat directly under you. Count "And three..."

82. Straighten both knees completely. Count "And four..." The arms, which began in Fifth Position Low, opened to the *demi-seconde* position during the *plié* and closed again to Fifth Position as the knees straightened.

85. Lean the body to the right, turning toward the audience. Arms remain in Fifth Position High. Count "Two and three..."

86. Open both arms outward and lower them to Fifth Position Low. At the same time lower the left heel to the floor, face front and raise the right foot to point in front of the ankle. Count "And four..."

83

84

PORT DE BRAS (por deh brah)

83. From a quick *demi-plié* spring up to Fifth Position on the *demi-pointes (sous-sous);* draw both feet together as you spring up, so that the feet are crossed and well turned out as you stand on the *demi-pointes*. (The position looks like one foot with two heels.) Raise the arms forward to Fifth Position Front. Count "And one..."

84. Stay on the *demi-pointes*, pulling the knees up tightly and raise the arms to Fifth Position High. Count "And..."

85

86

87   88   89   90

DÉVELOPPÉ À LA QUATRIÈME DEVANT
(deh-veh-loh-pay' ah lah caht-ree-em' deh-vahn)

87. *Passé* (pah-say). This means to pass the foot to a position at the knee in preparation for opening it in the développé. The right foot is strongly pointed at the little hollow of the supporting knee. Keep the right knee well turned out and the left knee tightly pulled up. The balance is forward over the ball of the supporting foot. Arms remain in Fifth Position Low. Count "And one…"

88. Press the right knee back and raise the right heel. At the same time raise the arms to Fifth Position in front. Keep the left knee very straight. Count "And…"

89. Stretch the right leg to its fullest length, tightening the knee. Keep the foot well pointed and the toes in alignment with the heel. Remember to remain lifted out of the hips. As the foot unfolds, the arms open outward to Second Position. Count "Two and three…" The knee should be straight on count "Two" and the pose is held for the third count.

90. Lower the toes of the right foot slowly to the floor and pause for a moment. Count "And four…"

91

91   92   93   94   95

DÉVELOPPÉ À LA SECONDE

91. Bring the right foot *sur le cou de pied* (sir luh coo deh pee-ay', "on the ankle") and lower both arms to Fifth Position Low. Count "And…"

92. *Passé.* Count "One…"

93. Without dropping the thigh take the foot out to the side. Remember not to allow the right hip to come out of place and not to sit into the left hip; remain centered. Don't twist the shoulders out of alignment. Raise arms to Fifth Position Front. "And…"

94. Stretch the right leg to its fullest length, tightening both knees. Keep the thigh well turned out and the toes strongly pointed. Remain well lifted. As the knee straightens, the arms open out to Second Position. Count "Two and three…" straightening the knee on "Two and holding the pose for the third count.

95. Lower the right foot slowly to the floor to point in *à la seconde à terre.* Count "And four…"

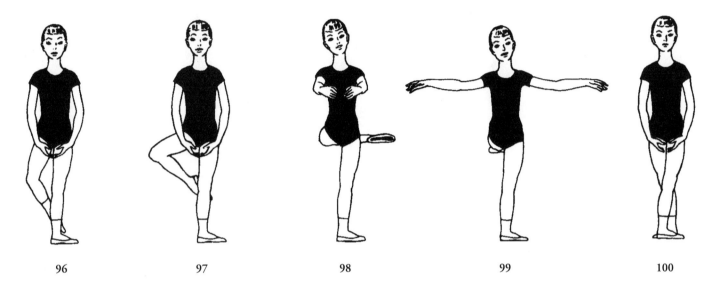

96   97   98   99   100

DÉVELOPPÉ À LA QUATRIÈME DERRIÈRE

96. Bring the right foot *sur le cou de pied, derrière* (on the ankle, in back). Count "And…"

97. *Passé.* Count "One…"

98. Without dropping the thigh carry the right knee back, crossing the leg in back of the body as much as possible without turning the shoulders. These should remain squarely front. Do not permit the knee to drop below the level of the foot. Raise the arms to Fifth Position in front. The weight of the body shifts forward slightly so that it continues to fall over the ball of the supporting foot. Count "And…"

99. Stretch the right leg to its fullest length, tightening the knee. Pull up the supporting knee at all times. Keep the lift in the ribs and the shoulders in alignment. As the knee straightens, the arms open outward to Second Position. Count "Two and three…" as in the other *développés.*

100. Lower the toes of the right foot slowly to the floor and slide the right foot into Fifth Position in back of the left. At the same time lower both arms to Fifth Position Low. Count "And four…"

The Basic Positions of the Body

There are certain basic poses and positions of the body that are absolutely essential for you to memorize, for it is on these poses and positions that most of our dancing is built. It is the turn of the shoulders, the inclination of the head, and the form of the arms that give style, life and interest to ballet movements. With these poses we begin to understand *line*. Line is the design the body makes in space. Balletic movement is based on line, so if you do not have a good sense of line you will never achieve beauty of movement.

You have already learned three basic position – *à la quatrième devant*, *à la seconde* and *à la quatrième derrière*. These positions are all taken *en face* (ahn fahss), or facing squarely to the front. To these we add the positions that are taken *en croisé* (ahn crwah-zay'), or crossed, and *en effacé* (ahn eh-fah-say'), or shaded. These are the positions that add quality and give a fuller meaning to the dance.

It is not easy to get the "feel" of these positions. Study the drawings carefully. Then try each pose in front of the mirror. Check the positions of your feet, your legs, your hips, your shoulders, your arms, and your head. When everything looks right, try to memorize the feel of the pose. Now turn away from the mirror and try to reproduce the pose correctly without looking at yourself.

94

CROISÉ DEVANT, À TERRE

(crwah-zay' deh-vahn', ah tair)

101. *Croisé devant* means "crossed in front" and gets its name from the position of the feet in this pose. *"à terre"* means "on the ground." A position is called *à terre* when the working leg is pointed on the floor.

Stand in Crossed Fourth Position, facing the lower left corner of the room. Fourth Position is called "Crossed Fourth" when the feet are separated from Fifth Position so that the toes are opposite the heels. Point the right foot in this position, open the arms to Third Position with the left arm high. Turn the head and incline it slightly to the right, and look straight out. Lean the upper body a little to the right without coming out of place or off center.

CROISÉ DEVANT, EN L'AIR

(crwah-zay' deh-vahn', ahn lair)

102. *En l'air* means "in the air," or raised off the ground. This is how the position looks when the leg is raised. When you can hold the pose correctly *à terre,* and feel well balanced, try raising the leg slowly off the floor. Correct line, turn-out, and placement are all more

101

102

important than the height of the leg. In practicing always remember this. The leg will go up easily when you have learned to hold yourself and to move correctly. Height of extension is the last step, not the first.

Practice all poses on both sides.

95

103   104   105–106   107

Exercise

103. Stand erect in Fifth Position with the right foot front, facing the lower left corner of the room. Hold the arms nicely in Fifth Position Low.

104. Slide the right foot front to a strong point in Fourth Position and at the same time raise both arms to Fifth Position Front. Count "One…"

105. Open both arms to Third Position with the left arm up. Keep the strong point in the right foot. Count "Two…"

106. "And three."

107. Return the right foot in Fifth Position in front of the left foot. At the same time open the left arm outward to Second Position, turn both wrists over, and lower the arms to Fifth Position Low.

Practice these four counts eight times with each foot. This exercise is meant to help you get the feel of the pose so that you fall into it naturally. It should be practiced in the same manner in each of the positions described in this book (although space does not permit us to illustrate it in all of the poses).

108

CROISÉ DERRIÈRE, à TERRE
(crwah-zay' dair-ee-air', ah tair)

108. *Croisé derrière* means, of course, "crossed in back." It is the opposite position to *croisé devant,* with the leg extended to the back instead of the front. Stand in Crossed Fourth Position with the right foot front, facing the lower left corner of the room, just as you began the *croisé devant* position. Both hips and both shoulders face the corner. Point the left foot in this position (the left foot now points to the upper right corner). Open both arms to Third Position with the right arm high. Bend the upper body slightly to the left. Incline the head to the left and look under the right arm to the audience.

CROISÉ DERRIÈRE, EN L'AIR
(crwah-zay' dair-ee-air', ahn lair)

109. Hold the body in this position as the leg is taken up, but shift the weight slightly toward the ball of the right foot. Practice the exercise on page 96 in *croisé derrière.*

109

À LA QUATRIÈME DEVANT, EN L'AIR
(ah lah caht-ree-em' deh-vahn', ahn lair)

111. The same position with the leg raised. Remember the rules of body placement. Practice the exercise on page 96 in *quatrième devant* position.

110

111

À LA QUATRIÈME DEVANT, À TERRE
(ah lah caht-ree-em' de vahn', ah tair)

110. This is the Fourth Position Front. Stand in Crossed Fourth Position with the right foot front, face *en face*, which means directly to the front. Point the right foot in Fourth Position. Open the arms to Second Position. Hold the head erect, the gaze straight forward.

112

À LA QUATRIÈME DERRIÈRE, EN L'AIR
(ah lah caht-ree-em' dair-ee-air', ahn lair)

113. The same position with the leg raised. Remember to take the upper body slightly forward as the leg goes up so that the balance remains over the ball of the right foot. Keep the back strong by lifting the ribs and pressing the shoulder blades down in the back. Practice the exercise on page 96 in the *quatrième derrière* position.

113

À LA QUATRIÈME DERRIÈRE, À TERRE
(ah lah caht-ree-em' dair-ee-air', ah tair)

112. This is the Fourth Position in the back. It is the opposite position to *à la quatrième devant.* Stand in Crossed Fourth Position, facing *en face* with the right foot front. Point the left foot in Fourth Position. Keep the weight of the body forward over the ball of the right foot. Open both arms to Second Position. Hold the head erect, the gaze straight forward. Don't forget to turn out the right leg and to point on the inside of the big toe of the left foot with the heel pressed down.

99

114

115

ÉCARTÉ DEVANT, À TERRE
(ay-car-tay' deh-vahn', ah tair)

The English meaning of *écarté* is "separated," or "thrown widely apart." *Écarté* is Second Position of the feet with the body facing the corner of the room instead of *en face,* or squarely front.

114. Face the lower left corner of the room. Stand in a good Second Position. Point the right foot in Second Position. Point the right foot in Second Position. (The right foot is now pointing to the lower right corner). Open both arms to Third Position with the right arm

high. Turn the head to the right and raise the chin a little so that you are looking up toward the palm of the right hand. Remember that in Second Position the feet are in line with each other.

ÉCARTÉ DEVANT, EN L'AIR
(ay-car-tay deh-vahn', ahn lair)

115. The balance is very difficult in this position. Don't come "out of placement" in order to raise the leg. Practice the exercise described on page 96 in *écarté* position.

116

117

ÉCARTÉ DERRIÈRE, À TERRE
(ay-car-tay' dair-ee-air', ah tair)

116. This is the opposite position to *écarté devant,* with the leg extended back instead of front. Stand in Second Position, facing the lower left corner of the room. Point the left foot in Second Position (left foot points to upper left corner). Open the arms to Third Position with the left arm up. Bend the body, from the waist, to the right. Turn the head to the right and look to the lower right corner.

ÉCARTÉ DERRIÈRE, EN L'AIR
(ay-car-tay dair-ee-air', ahn lair)

117. Remain in this position and raise the left leg. This pose requires good balance, so think about all the facts of body placement before you attempt it. Practice *écarté derrière* according to the exercise described on page 96.

101

118

EFFACÉ DEVANT, À TERRE
(eh-fah-say' deh-vahn', ah tair)

The English meaning of *effacé* is "shaded." The pose gets its name from the fact that the body is turned so that part of it is shaded from view. *Effacé* is an open or uncrossed position of the leg.

118. Face the lower right corner of the room. Stand in Crossed Fourth Position (Fourth Position out of Fifth), with the right foot front. Both hips and both shoulders face the right corner. Point the right foot in this position. Open the arms to Third Position with the left arm high. Incline the head to the left and look straight out. Lean the upper body slightly back. Take care that the pointing leg is well turned out.

EFFACÉ DEVANT, EN L'AIR
(eh-fah-say' deh-vahn', ahn lair)

119. Raise the leg without twisting the shoulders or the hips around. Practice the exercise described on page 96 in the *effacé devant* position.

119

121. Hold the body in this position and raise the left leg. Shift the weight slightly toward the ball of the foot as the leg is raised. Practice the exercise described on page 96 in the *effacé derrière* position.

120

EFFACÉ DERRIÈRE, À TERRE
(eh-fah-say' dair-ee-air', ah tair)

120. This is the opposite position to *effacé devant,* with the leg extended back instead of front. Stand in Open Fourth Position (Fourth Position taken out of First Position), facing the lower right corner of the room. Point the left foot in Fourth Position. Open the arms to Third Position with the left arm up. Lean the upper body slightly to the right, incline the head to the right, and look under the left arm.

121

ÉPAULÉ, À TERRE
(ay-pol-ay', ah tair)

The English meaning of *épaulé* is "shouldered." The pose gets its name from the oblique angle of the body in an arabesque position. *Épaulé* is the Second Arabesque (see page 108), taken at an angle to the audience instead of in profile.

122. The feet are in the same position as in *éffacé derrière,* that is, an Open Fourth Position, facing the corner of the room. Stand in Open Fourth Position (Fourth Position out of First), with the left foot front, facing the lower left corner of the room. Point the right foot in this position. Raise the arms to Second Position. Turn the shoulders so that the right arm extends forward to the lower left corner and the left arm extends back to the upper right corner. Turn the palms down so that they face the floor. Incline the head to the right, and look straight out.

122   123

ÉPAULÉ, EN L'AIR
(ay-pol-ay', ahn lair)

123. Raise the foot off the floor without changing the position of the legs or shoulders. Practice the exercise described on page 96 in *épaulé* position.

104

À LA SECONDE, EN L'AIR
(ah lah seh-cohnd', ahn lair)

125. The same position with the leg raised. Be well centered and keep the right hip down as the leg goes up. Practice the exercise described on page 96 in *à la seconde* position.

124

125

À LA SECONDE, À TERRE
(ah lah seh-cohnd', ah tair)

124. This is Second Position of the feet facing *en face*, or squarely front. The arms, too, are held in Second Position. Watch that the arms remain round, that they are not held too high, or with one higher than the other.

Arabesques

(ah-rah-besk')

The arabesque is one of the basic poses of ballet. Among the ancient Moors and Greeks arabesque was a name given to an ornament of fantastic and geometric design. In ballet the name has been applied to certain poses to express their grace and charm.

Basically the arabesque is a long, flowing line made by standing on one leg while the other extends behind. The arms, too, extend the pose to make the longest possible line between finger tips and toe tips. Lastly, the head must always be in harmony with the line of the body.

The arabesque may be done with the supporting knee perfectly straight or in *demi-plié* position, but the raised leg must always be stretched, with its knee straight.

The basic pose of the arabesque has an infinite number of varieties that can be made by changing an arm position or the direction of the body. In this book we take up five basic arabesque poses. All other arabesques are derived from these five.

126

FIRST ARABESQUE, À TERRE

126. Stand in First Position, facing the right wall of the room. Check yourself for posture and placement. Slide the left foot back to a strong point in Open Fourth Position. Keep both shoulders facing squarely to the right wall. Raise the right arm to shoulder height. Keep it well stretched but not stiff; palm faces downward to the floor. Raise the left arm to shoulder height to Second Position; now press it back easily as far as it will go without strain and without turning the shoulders, and turn the palm down to face the floor. Hold the head erect and look straight out over the tips of the fingers. Let the hands stretch out fully, but keep the correct grouping of the fingers.

106

127

FIRST ARABESQUE

127. When you are able to stand well in *arabesque à terre,* with good balance and a strong feeling in your back, you are ready to try the full position with the raised leg.

Keep the good lift of the ribs and press the shoulder blades down well in the back. Now, as the leg is slowly raised, allow the body to lean forward a little from the hip joint so that the upper body is held over the toes of the supporting foot. Keep the arch in the back, try to raise the leg to 90° or the height of the hips. Arms and hands remain as in *arabesque à terre.* The head, too. Do not permit your body to roll or lean to the right. Practice this pose on both sides.

107

128

129

SECOND ARABESQUE, À TERRE

128. *Second Arabesque* is a line similar to First Arabesque except that the line is formed by the leg and corresponding arm rather than the opposite arm.

Stand in First Position, Facing the right wall. Point the left foot back in an Open Fourth Position. Raise both the arms to Second Position. Turn the shoulders so that the left arm extends forward from the shoulder to the right wall and the right arm extends back toward the opposite wall. Both palms are facing downward to the floor, both shoulders are pressed down low. The head is inclined to the left, look over the left shoulder to the audience. Try to achieve this line without any sense of strain.

SECOND ARABESQUE

129. Raise the leg, remembering all that we spoke about in First Arabesque. Keep the line in the shoulders and do not permit the back arm to drop. Take care not to allow the left knee to bend and keep the leg well opened from the hip. Practice this arabesque on both sides.

130   131

THIRD ARABESQUE

131. Follow the rules for First Arabesque. You should feel a strong pull up from the floor in the supporting leg, with the thigh muscles in both legs working hard to pull the knees straight. This not only makes for good form, it also helps you with your balance. Practice this arabesque on both sides.

THIRD ARABESQUE, À TERRE

130. This is an arabesque similar to the other two, but both arms are extended forward in opposition to the leg.

Stand in First Position, facing the right wall of the room. Slide the left foot directly back to point in an Open Fourth Position. Raise both arms forward, with the right arm a little above shoulder level and the left arm at shoulder level. Both the palms face downward to the floor, fingers stretched and hands lifted slightly to extend the movement. Watch that the grouping of the fingers remains simple and correct. The head is very slightly raised, the eyes look out over the top of the right hand.

132. Don't do this!

132

109

FOURTH
ARABESQUE, À TERRE

133. This arabesque is taken *en croisé.* That is, the legs appear to be in a crossed position when viewed from the audience. Another thing that makes this arabesque different from the first three is that the supporting knee is bent in a *demi-plié.*

Stand in Fifth Position with the left foot front, facing the lower right corner of the room; both shoulders and both hips face the corner. Slide the right foot directly back to a strong point in Fourth Position (the right foot points to the upper left corner). Raise the right arm and extend it from the shoulder toward the lower

133

134

right corner with the palm facing down. *Plié* with the left knee, keeping the heel firmly on the floor; arch the back very strongly. Lower the right shoulder slightly and incline the head to the right. Look straight out at the audience.

FOURTH ARABESQUE

134. This is a difficult position to do for many reasons and will require much practice. As the leg is raised, push back from the waist, maintaining the strongly arched back. The

leg in the air must be well turned out and the knee very straight. The supporting foot must also be well turned out, the supporting knee bent directly over the toes. The weight of the body falls over the knee onto the ball of the supporting foot. This is important, because if you allow the weight to fall back into the heel you will not be able to balance. The leg must be held at 90° or straight out from the hip. Arms, head, and shoulders as in 133. Practice this arabesque on both sides.

135

FIFTH ARABESQUE

136. All of the rules for Fourth Arabesque also hold true for Fifth Arabesque. In arching the back do not permit an air of strained effort to show. The pose must look easy and fluid. Practice this arabesque on both sides.

136

FIFTH ARABESQUE, À TERRE

135. Fifth Arabesque is similar to Fourth Arabesque except for the positions of the arms and head.

Stand in Fifth Position with the left foot front, facing the lower right corner of the room; both shoulders and both hips face the corner. Slide the right foot directly back to a strong point in Fourth Position (the right foot points to the upper left corner). Raise both arms as in Third Arabesque, extending them to the lower right corner. Incline the head to the left shoulder and look straight out to the audience. *Plié* with the left knee, keeping the left heel firmly on the floor. Arch the back very strongly.

The Attitudes
(ah-tee-tood')

137

The poses in ballet that are known as the *attitudes* are among the loveliest poses of ballet and are the most difficult to do well. The pose was inspired by the famous statue of Mercury by Jean Bologne. You have probably seen pictures of this statue in your mythology books. Here are four basic *attitude* positions. Practice them on both sides.

ATTITUDE CROISÉE
(ah-tee-tood' crwah-zay')

137. Stand in Fifth Position with the left foot front, facing the lower right corner of the room. Arms in Fifth Position Low. Slide the right foot back to a strong point in Fourth Position and at the same raise both arms to Fifth Position Front. Raise the right leg with the knee bent sharply at a right angle and arch the back, pushing the seat forward. At the same time open the arms to Third Position with the right arm high. As the knee is brought up, press it to the left so that the leg crosses the body in back, showing the foot and calf muscle to the audience. Keep the knee lifted and the foot level with it. It is a bad fault to permit the knee to drop below the level of the foot. Pull the right shoulder well forward and press both shoulders down firmly. Keep the right hand a little forward so that you can see it without throwing the head back. Incline the head to the left and look toward the audience. Hold the pose as long as you can, then straighten the knee, point the foot down on the floor, and slide it into Fifth Position.

138

139

ATTITUDE CROISÉE (rear view)

138. This drawing shows you how the knee must be bent and brought back across the body. It also shows the alignment of foot to knee.

ATTITUDE EFFACÉE (ah-tee-tood' eh-fahs-say')

139. Stand in First Position, facing the lower left corner of the room with the arms in Fifth Position Front. Slide the right foot back to a point in Fourth Position and raise the arms to Third Position, right arm high. The position is now *effacée derrière, à terre* (120). Raise the right leg, with the knee bent, to an angle of 90°. The knee is not bent as sharply as in *attitude croisée*. It is only half bent and allows the lower part of the leg to be seen by the audience. The body leans very slightly toward the supporting leg. The head is turned so that the eyes look into the palm of the right hand. Hold this pose as long as you can, then straighten the knee, lower the pointed foot to the floor, and return it to First Position. Throughout the exercise keep the supporting knee pulled up tight.

140

141

ATTITUDE DEVANT
(ah-tee-tood' deh-vahn')

141. The position of the body in this pose is the same as in *croisé devant* (102), but the raised knee is bent and forced out so that the heel is raised as much as possible in this position. Arms and head as in *croisé devant*.

142. Don't do this!

142

ATTITUDE ÉPAULÉE
(ah-tee-tood' ay-pol-ay')

140. Stand in Fifth Position with the left foot front, facing the upper left corner of the room. Arms in Fifth Position Low. Slide the right foot back to point in Fourth Position and at the same time raise both arms to Fifth Position Front. Raise the right knee and the arms into *attitude croisée* position. Turn the head to the right, raise the chin, and look into the palm of the right hand. Hold this pose as long as you can, then straighten the knee, lower the pointed foot to the floor, close into Fifth Position.

III
Basic Allegro Steps

Note To Students

The following are the basic elevation and connecting steps of ballet. By "elevation" we mean steps that are taken off the ground by leaping or springing. It is natural that this should be a favorite part of the class, for the basic steps of ballet are to the dance what words are to a language. With these steps we make *enchaînements* or *combinations*. That is, we put them together, in a series, in various combined forms to develop balletic phrases and sentences just as we put words together to form sentences in speech.

To perform these basic steps well—that is, with ease, control, and balletic form—much strength is needed in the feet, legs and back.

Ease means that while you are doing all of these things you do not show any strain by hunching your shoulders, straining your neck cords, or tensing your arms or hands.

Control means that you are able to jump to the necessary height and then alight gracefully, softly, and lightly on the ground without any loss of posture or poise.

Balletic form means that when you leave the ground in a leaping or springing step you are able to point your feet, turn your legs well outward, hold your back very straight, hold your arms gracefully in a given position, control your head in a given position, and exhibit good line in your poses in the air.

In order to perform the steps of *allegro* correctly, there is much preliminary work to develop the strength needed. This strength is developed first through consistent practice of the exercises of barre work. That is the function of the barre exercises—to develop the strength you need in your feet, legs and back and to make your tendons and muscles elastic and springy. These same exercises must also be practiced away from the barre in order to develop your sense of balance.

You have been practicing your barre work faithfully and you have also been practicing your center barre and *adagio* exercises. You are progressing in your classwork and you are eager to practice, at home, the steps and combinations of steps your teacher is now giving you in the classroom.

There are two parts to your *allegro* practice. The first is to practice each step individually for perfection of execution. This is very important in itself, for in an *enchaînement* each step must be as perfect as a little jewel in order for the effect to be as sparking as *allegro* dancing demands. The second part is to work on the *enchaînements* given you by your teacher. This is important to develop your memory powers so that you can connect one step to another easily. The ability to do this comes from being able to think one step ahead each time, and, to do this, the mind must be made more quick and agile by exercising thought just as you do your muscles.

NEVER practice these jumping steps without first warming up the muscles and tendons of your legs *with at least fifteen or twenty minutes of good barre work.* Start with *pliés*, proceed to *battements tendus* and *dégagés*, finish up with *grands battements* and *relevés* to get your muscles toned up and your tendons stretched. Work carefully and slowly. Trying to jump with "cold" legs and feet may cause you to injure yourself seriously by twisting or spraining your ankle or forefoot or damaging your Achilles tendon, which is at the back of your ankle. A professional dancer would not practice *allegro* or dance on the stage without this preliminary warm-up of barre practice. You, too, must be guided by the wisdom and experience of the professional dancer.

In practicing the steps remember that your arms, your shoulders, and your head are a very important part of your equipment as a dancer. Here is where all our practice of *port de bras, épaulement,* and directions of the body in space become of practical use. The movements of the arms and hands, the turn of the shoulders and head, must be coordinated with those of the feet and legs, for they embellish the movement and show the grace of the dancer. Sometimes we merely hold our arms still, but they must be held in a correct position with no tension or strain. At other times we move our arms in coordination and harmony with the legs, and they must move gracefully and flowingly, not in stiff, jerky movements. This is most difficult to do well and requires infinite care in practice. The same is true of the head and shoulders. At times we hold the head erect and face directly front; at other times we turn our shoulders to *croisé* or *effacé* and incline the head. This gives variety, interest, and artistic quality to our jumping.

Of course you cannot master everything at once. Begin by getting good command of the legs and feet, but as soon as possible try to add the arm movements and then the *épaulement*. It takes many years of striving to achieve the perfection you hope to attain.

Allegro

Allegro is an Italian word meaning "glad" or "merry." In music it denotes a quick and lively tempo. In ballet it is used as a general term for all of the steps of elevation—that is, jumping steps—which are generally performed to 2/4, 3/4, 4/4, 3/8, or 6/8 rhythm played at a lively tempo. All of the steps described in this section are the simple basic steps of ballet and come under the general term of *allegro*.

Another word you need to know well is *ballon* (bah-lohn'). *Ballon* is an essential part of *allegro* dancing. We speak of a dancer as having "good *ballon*" or as having "no *ballon*." *Ballon* in ballet means a bouncy quality in jumping. It means that the dancer bounds up from the floor, stays a moment in the air, and alights from the jump with lightness and elasticity like a rubber ball that bounces across the floor. A dancer who has no *ballon* gives the impression of being heavy and bound to the floor, the dancer who has good *ballon* gives the impression of being light and in flight. So, you see, good *ballon* is essential to the dancer.

You must also realize that no dancer is born with good *ballon*, although some people are naturally able to jump higher than others. Good *ballon* is the result of proper technical training. It is achieved through the correct use of the insteps of the feet and the elasticity of the knees and Achilles tendons.

By studying the next eight pages carefully and then putting into practice the theory explained there you will acquire good *ballon*. Remember that the faithful practices of your barre exercises—*demi-pliés, battements tendus, dégagés,* and *frappés,* as well as *relevés*—is your best aid in acquiring better *ballon* in your jumps.

The Various Levels of the Foot in Jumping

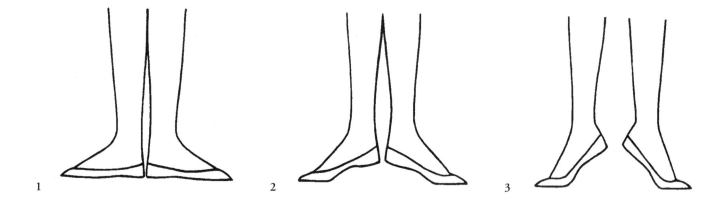

1 2 3

1. *Pied à terre* (pee-ayd' ah tair). The foot "on flat." In springing upward we always begin from a position with the heels or heel pressed firmly against the floor, depending on whether we are springing from two feet or one foot.

2. *Pied à quart* (pee-ayd' ah kar'). The foot at Quarter Point. We push away from the floor by forcefully pushing up through the insteps. As we begin this push the heel comes up first.

3. *Pied à demi* (pee-ayd' ah deh-mee'). Also called *sur la demi-pointe* (soor la deh-mee' pwahnt). We continue to push up through the ball of the foot.

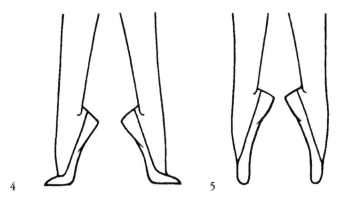

4   5

In descending from a jump we reverse this action of the foot or feet. The toes remain pointed until almost the instant of contact with the floor (5), the first contact with the floor is high on the three-quarter point (4), we roll down into the under part of the ball of the foot (3), we continue to roll down the metatarsal arch, controlling the descent of the heel (2), we complete the landing with the heel pressed firmly onto the floor, all of the toes straight on the floor, the arch well lifted (1).

4. *Pied à trios quart* (pee-ayd' ah trwah kar). The foot at three-quarter point. We continue to push up through the instep.

5. *Pied à pointe* (pee-ayd' ah pwahnt). Also called *sur la pointe*. The Full Point Position. In jumping our last contact with the floor is the tips of our toes as we push them downward into a strong point the instant we leave the floor.

In working on *adagio* and on turns, as well as in jumping, it is necessary for a dancer to have complete control and balance at any level of the foot shown here. These levels of balance are used in different ways for various purposes. Of course the Full Point Position is the one girls use in toe dancing or *en pointe*.

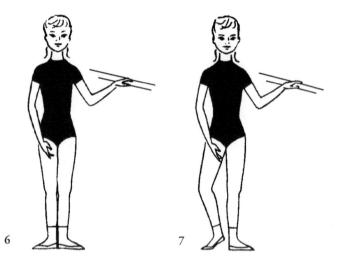

6   7

EXERCISE

Practice this exercise at the barre. It will help you to acquire good *ballon*.

6. Ready to begin. Stand in First Position holding the barre with the left hand. The weight of the body is evenly distributed over both feet. Remember that, in ballet, balance is over the balls of the feet so that, although your heels are held firmly against the floor, they do not carry the weight of the body. You should feel as though you could raise the heels off the ground at any time you wish to do so. Think of all the rules of good body placement. Hold the right arm in the Fifth Position Low.

7. Raise your right heel, pushing down into the ball of the foot. Count "And."

8. Roll upward through the toes of the right foot, pushing

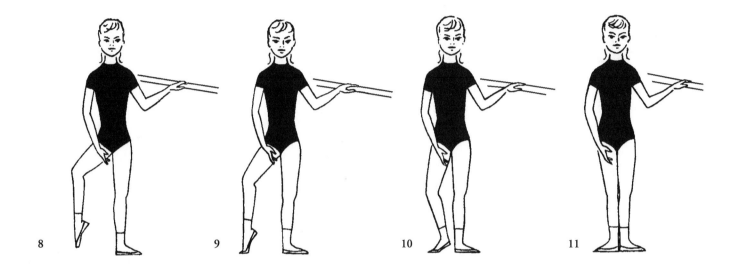

8   9   10   11

forcefully against and from the floor until the pointed toes are pointed a few inches above the floor. At the same time transfer the weight of the body to the left foot. (Take care not to sit into your left hip.) Count "A one."

9. Lower the right foot until the tips of the toes touch the floor. Count "And."

10. Roll down the toes to the ball of the foot. Count "A."

11. Roll down the instep to the heel, returning the foot to First Position. Allow the weight of the body to equalize itself over both feet. Count "Two."

Practice this exercise sixteen times with the right foot, then turn around and practice it sixteen times with the left foot. You may also practice this exercise from Second Position instead of First Position.

The Importance of the Plié in Jumping

While it is necessary to acquire the correct action of the insteps of the feet in order to jump lightly and descend softly, the correct use of the feet alone is not sufficient to make us jump well.

The *plié* is of equal importance with the use of the insteps to give lightness and bounce to our leaping and springing steps. Without this springy action of the knees it is impossible to jump high, to bound, or to leap.

Prove it to yourself. Stand on both feet with the knees straight. Now try to jump off the floor without bending your knees as you take off or as you land. You see how impossible it is to get any elevation off the ground—and in landing with stiff knees the result is bumpy, jerky, and jarring to the spine.

It is the soft bending of the knees as the heels are lowered to the ground that gives smoothness to our jumping.

The most important part of learning to jump well is to begin a jump with a *demi-plié*, the heels pressed firmly into the floor, and to finish the jump with a *demi-plié*, the heels again pressed firmly into the floor. There are several reasons for the important of this point.

The Achilles tendon, which is at the back of the ankle at the heel, is a very powerful factor in jumping. If the tendon is not

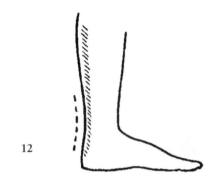

12

stretched fully, by a good *demi-plié*, each time you begin or end a jump it becomes stiff and thickened instead of elastic and springy. Once it becomes stiff it is impossible to execute a good *demi-plié* with the heels properly pressed into the floor, and almost impossible ever to stretch it out. The dancer, in such a case, has no real control over the body in landing from a jump because the ankles are wobbly without the firm pressure of the heels against the floor. The ankles may easily be sprained or even broken by such lack of control.

Furthermore, it is this push-off of the heels from the floor that gives the power to jump high, and it is the soft descent into the heels that makes landing light.

12. The Achilles tendon.

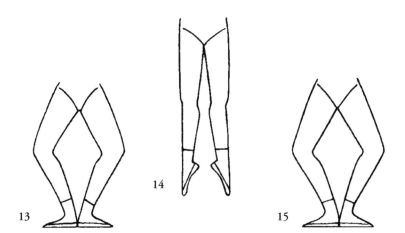

13

14

15

DON'T DO THIS!

16. Incorrect position in landing from a jump. The knees have been allowed to fall in front of the arches causing the feet to roll in. This will certainly cause damage to the feet as the strain of taking the full weight of the body in landing is too much for the arches in this position.

17. OOF! Don't ever land from a jump with stiff knees.

13. Preparation for a spring from the floor.

14. Position of the legs and feet in the air. The turn-out must be maintained at the hips and the feet always pointed as soon as they leave the ground.

15. Finish of the jump. Knees pointed back and out directly over the toes. Feet are holding the floor with big toe, little toe, and heel.

16.–17. DON'T DO THIS!

16

17

How to Keep Your Jumping Light

Dancers should be seen and not heard. Of course. Nothing is more ridiculous than a dancer who lands heavily and noisily from a jump. A dancer must give the impression of flight—of being air-borne, not earth-bound.

We have already spoken about two things that make jumping light. One is the correct use of the insteps and the other is the correct use of *demi-pliés*.

There is another contributing factor to jumping lightly. This is the proper lift of the ribs and the pulling upward of the body out of the hips. In other words, at all times, the weight of the body must be pulled upward and distributed through the body rather than resting entirely upon the feet.

If you have been faithful about working on your posture and body placement, you will have no trouble with this. See Section I, *Basic Exercises at the Barre.*

When the landing is made from a jump, the weight of the body must be controlled by this upward lift. If the back is held strong and straight (by lifting the ribs, pulling the shoulder blades down, and keeping the buttocks under), as we touch the floor and roll down into the proper *plié* the landing will be noiseless. If, on the contrary, the back is allowed to weaken and the body

to "break" as the landing is made, the result will be noisy even if the insteps, heels, and knees are working properly. Besides it looks dreadful to see such loss of control in the back and spoils the entire artistic effect of the jump.

Proper breathing is another big factor in learning to jump lightly. We dancers must learn breath control just as singers do. The important rule for breathing in jumping is to "breathe with the effort." That is, inhale as you spring upward and expel the air easily and slowly in alighting. The higher the jump the deeper the breath.

The eyes, too, are important in jumping, as is the head. If you want to jump high and look good in the air, keep your chin up and look straight out. Never hang your head. Don't look down at the floor. Keep your shoulders down. Hunching them does not help to get you up higher, it merely makes you look awkward.

Timing is a very important part of jumping too. When the music is slow, we must jump higher than when the music is fast. We, therefore, must be guided by the music in determining how high to jump in any step. If we jump too high and do not keep the tempo, the jump will look heavy no matter how high it is. And, of course, since rhythm is such a basic part of dancing, no one who is unmusical can ever be called a dancer.

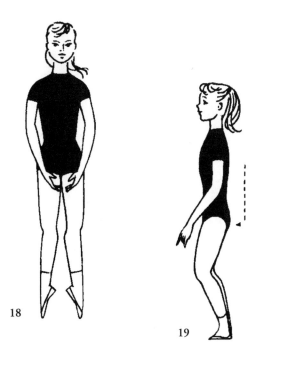

18

19

DON'T DO THIS!

20. Heels off the floor in a preparatory *plié* or in alighting from a jump.
21. Ribs dropped, shoulders hunched, buttocks sticking out, in the air.
22. "Break" in landing, ribs dropped, buttocks sticking out.

DON'T DO THIS!

20   21   22

18. While in the air keep your back straight by lifting your ribs, pulling your shoulder blades down and under, lifting up out of the hips, and keeping your buttocks under.
19. On the floor, in preparing for a jump and in alighting from a jump, keep your back straight and your buttocks under.

Temps Levé on Two Feet

(tahn leh-vay')

The translation of "*temps levé*" is "elevated time." When the word *temps* is used as part of the name of a step, it refers to the preparatory beat of the music before the actual beat. Therefore the name of this step stems from the fact that we are in the air on the preparatory beat finishing on the floor on the actual beat of the music.

Temps levé on two feet may be taken from First Position, Second Position or Fourth Position.

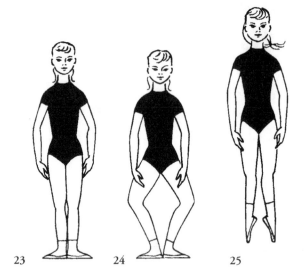

23   24   25

TEMPS LEVÉ IN FIRST POSITION

23. Ready to begin. Stand erect, feet in First Position, arms in First Position.

24. *Demi-plié.* Remember to keep your head erect and your eyes open, looking straight out. Think of your back. Press your heels firmly into the floor.

25. Push off the ground, forcing your knees to straighten and your toes to push down into a strong point. Do not throw your legs apart or bring them together, keep them well turned outward from the hips. Remember to keep your back straight and strong and to keep your buttocks tightened. The arms remain in First Position.

132

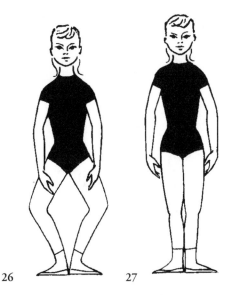

26   27

26. Finish in a good demi-plié with both heels pressed firmly into the floor. Your back must be strong as steel! Keep your head up, don't roll in on your arches, press your knees back and out over your toes, don't stick your seat out in back. Remember to touch the floor with the toes first and then to roll down into the heels.

27. Straighten both knees.

Practice the *temps levé* in this manner eight times. If you are practicing to music, use a 2/4 rhythm. Alight from the jump on the first beat of the measure and straighten the knees on the second beat.

You may also practice this step without straightening the knees between jumps. Hold the *plié* position for the second beat of the measure and spring up into the next *temps levé* from this *plié*. Both ways are valuable for practice. The first way will make you conscious of the action of your knees and the necessity for keeping them springy; the second way will give you time to think of holding the back strong, the knees turned out, the feet straight, and the chin up as you struggle to keep your heels pressed into the floor.

After you have practice this *temps levé* in the First Position, practice it the same way with the feet and the arms in Second Position.

Practice the *temps levé* with the feet in Fourth Position eight times with the right foot front, eight times with the left foot front. Hold the arms in Fourth Position High (see Section II, *Basic Center Exercises*) with the raised arm on the side opposite the front foot.

Temps Levé from Two Feet to One Foot

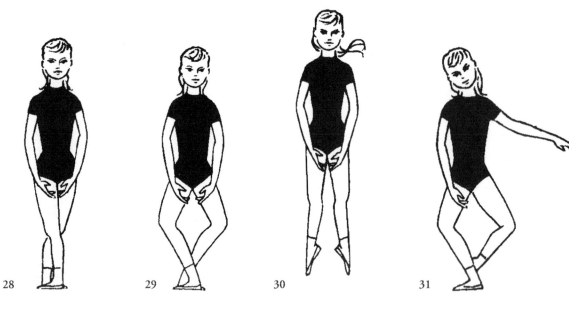

28   29   30   31

DERRIÈRE (dair-ee-air') (in back)

28. Ready to begin. Stand in Fifth Position with the right foot front. Arms in Fifth Position Low.

29. *Demi-plié.*

30. Spring straight up into the air, point both feet, straighten both knees. Arms remain in Fifth Position Low, head erect.

31. Alight on the right foot, rolling down into a *demi-plié* and at the same time raise the left foot *sur le cou de pied derrière* (sur leh coo deh pee-ay') (in back of ankle). At the instant you land raise the left arm to *demi-seconde* Position, and incline the head to the right. Remember, back straight, seat under, all the toes on the floor, heel on the floor, knee well bent and pushed out over the toes, point the left foot strongly and press its heel against the calf muscle of the right leg.

DEVANT (de-vahn') (in front)

32. Ready to begin as in Number 28.

33. *Demi-plié.*

34. Spring straight up into the air, point both feet, straighten both knees. Arms remain in Fifth Position Low, head erect.

35. Alight on the left foot, at the same time raise the right foot *sur le cou de pied devant* (in front of the left ankle). At the instant you land raise the right arm to *demi-seconde* Position, and incline the head to the left. Hold the right foot close to the left shinbone and point it strongly.

Practice the temps levé from two feet to one foot in combination with the assemblé (see page 146). Use a 2/4 rhythm.

Stand in Fifth Position, left foot front. Do a *temps levé,* raising the right foot *sur le cou de pied derrière*, count "And one." Hold the *plié* position for count "And two." Take an *assemblé dessus* (page 146) with the right foot, count "And one." Hold the *plié* position for count "And two." Repeat the *temps levé* and the *assemblé* with the left foot. Take the entire step alternating right foot and left four times.

Hold the arms in *demi-seconde* Position until you feel sure of the feet and are able to do the steps well, then add the arm movements to your practice.

You may also practice this step in reverse. Take your temps levé sur le cou de pied devant and your assemblé dessous (page 148).

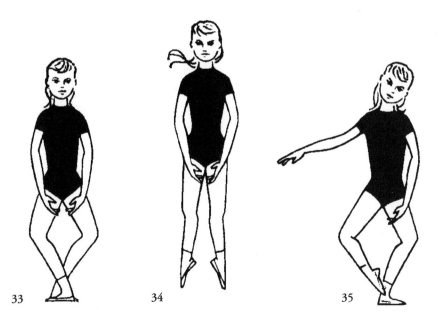

33   34   35

135

Temps Levé on One Foot

37

36

38

This temps levé may be done with the raised foot held either *sur le cou de pied derrière* or *devant*.

DERRIÈRE

36. Ready to begin. Stand on the right foot. In a *demi-plié* with the left foot raised to a pointed position behind the right calf muscle. Remember, hold the floor firmly with the big toe, little toe, and heel, keep the back straight, both knees well turned outward. Hold the left arm in Fifth Position Low and the right arm in *demi-seconde* Position (Cecchetti Third Position), incline the head to the left.

37. Spring straight up into the air, pointing the right foot strongly. Keep the head inclined, the back straight and strong, and the arms in the same position. Count "And."

38. Come down into the soft *plié* on the right foot rolling down the instep to the heel. Keep your back strong, don't "break." Hold the left foot in its pointed position behind the right calf muscle, press both knees back and out over the toes, retain the position of the arms and the inclination of the head. Count "One."

136

DEVANT

39–41. To execute this *temps levé sur le cou de pied devant,* raise the left foot in front of the right leg at the center of the shinbone. Hold the right arm in Fifth Position Low, the left arm in *demi-seconde* Position and the head inclined to the right.

Practice the *temps levé* on the right foot eight times with the left foot *sur le cou de pied derrière.* Then practice it eight times on the left foot with the right foot *sur le cou de pied derrière.* Practice eight times on each foot with the *sur le cou de pied devant* position. Use a 2/4 rhythm played slowly. Spring into the air, each time, on the preparatory beat and *plié* well on the actual beat of the music.

You may also practice this *temps levé* in combination with the *jeté* (pages 150–153). Use the same 2/4 rhythm. Take a *jeté derrière* ("And one"); *temps levé* with the raised foot *sur le cou de pied derrière* ("And two"). Repeat the *jeté* and *temps levé* on the other foot. Do this combination eight times. This step will travel forward. You may also travel backward by taking *jeté devant* and your *temps levé* with the foot held *sur le cou de pied devant.*

39   40   41

Soubresaut

(soo-breh-soh')

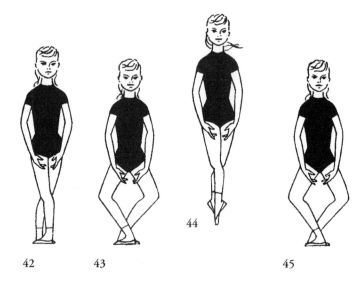

S oubresaut is like the *temps levé* on two feet except that it is done in Fifth Position.

42. Ready to begin. Stand in Fifth Position with the right foot front, head erect, look straight out, arms in Fifth Position Low.

43. *Demi-plié*. Count "And."

44. Spring straight up into the air with both feet. Point strongly, cross the right foot over the left, pressing them tightly against each other. Hold your back straight and strong, your head erect, look straight out. Keep the arms in Fifth Position Low. Count "A."

45. Come down into *demi-plié* in a good Fifth Position. The toes of both feet touch the floor at the same instant. Hold your back straight as you roll down the insteps and press your heels firmly into the floor. Count "One."

This is the simplest form of *soubresaut*. The arms may be used in many ways in this step, but the best way for you to practice it is with the arms in Fifth Position Low. Your teacher will teach you other ways to hold your arms as you progress in your training.

Practice this step to a 2/4 rhythm. Spring up on the preparatory beat, finish on the first beat of the measure and hold the *demi-plié* for the second beat. Practice this step eight times with the right foot front, then eight times with the left foot front.

Changement de Pieds

(shanzh-mahn' deh pee-ay')

Changement de pieds means "changing of the feet." This step gets its name from the fact that we begin in Fifth Position with either the right or the left foot front, spring into the air, and change the feet as we descend from the jump so that the foot that was in front finished behind, again in Fifth Position.

46. Ready to begin. Stand in Fifth Position with right foot front, head erect, arms in Fifth Position Low. Remember to keep body well lifted out of hips and shoulder blades pulled down low as you do this step.

47. *Demi-plié.* Keep the weight equally distributed over both feet. Count "And."

48. Spring straight up into the air, pushing down hard through the knees and toes. Press the heels forward, open the legs slightly. Count "A."

49. As you descend from the jump, change your feet so that the left foot finished in front of the right foot in Fifth Position. Be sure to finish in a good *demi-plié* with all of the toes and both heels firmly on the floor. Count "One."

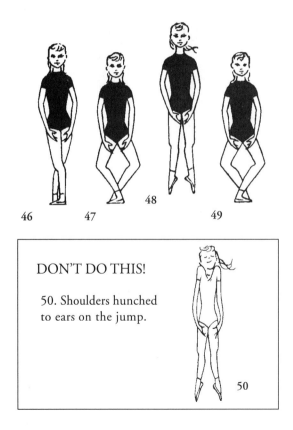

Practice this step to a 2/4 rhythm. Spring into the air on the preparatory beat and alight in the *plié* on the first beat of the measure. Hold the second beat in the good *plié* position. Do this eight times, later sixteen times. Remember your breath control, inhale deeply as you spring up, exhale easily as you descend.

DON'T DO THIS!

50. Shoulders hunched to ears on the jump.

Échappé Sauté

(ay-shah-pay' soh-tay')

The name of this step comes from the French verb "*échapper*," which means "to escape," and "*sauter*," which means "to jump." The legs "escape" from Fifth Position to Second Position on the jump.

51. Ready to begin. Stand in Fifth Position with the right foot front. Face directly front. Hold the head erect, the back straight, the body well lifted up out of the hips, the shoulder blades well down and under, the arms in Fifth Position Low.

52. *Demi-plié.* Remember to open the knees out over the toes, to hold the floor firmly with the big toes, little toes, and heels, and the weight equal over both feet. Count "And."

53. Spring straight up into the air, pulling the body up from the hips and forcing the knees and toes down very straight and pointed. The right foot is crossed over the left (*soubresaut,* page 138). As you spring up, raise the arms to Fifth Position Front and look straight front. Count "And.'

54. As you begin to descend from the jump, throw both legs apart to Second Position, keeping both knees straight and both feet pointed.

55. Finish the jump quietly in Second Position, *demi-plié.*

56   57   58

Both arms open out to Second Position as you descend. As you alight, turn the head to the right, looking to the right side of the room. Take care not to bring the feet in toward each other as you alight, but keep the same wide Second Position you had in the air. Remember not to bend forward as you touch the floor, hold the body well up out of the hips. Press the knees back and out over the toes. Count "One."

56. Spring straight up into the air,

pointing the feet in Second Position. Count "And."

57. As you descend from the jump bring the legs together into Fifth Position with the left foot in front of the right. Count "A."

58. Finish in *demi-plié* in Fifth Position, left foot front. Lower the arms to Fifth Position as you alight and turn the head to look straight front. Count "Two.

Practice the *échappé sauté* eight times to a slow 2/4 rhythm, alternating right foot, then left foot, front. In the beginning it is wise to practice this step with the holding of the *plié* on the second beat of each measure so that you hold the *plié* in Second Position and the *plié* in Fifth Position each time. Later it can be practiced without this hold.

It is wise, too, to practice the feet alone without the arm or head movements until you can do the footwork correctly. Keep the arms in Fifth Position Low throughout.

When you add the arm movements, you will notice that this is the *port de bras*, which you have been practicing standing still. See Section II, *Basic Center Exercises*. Now you can begin to understand how important it is to practice your *port de bras* so that your arms will move gracefully as you jump. Be sure that your arm movements do not become jerky because of the effort you are making with your legs and feet.

Glissade

(glee-sahd')

The name of this step comes from the French verb *glisser* which means "to slide" or "to glide." There are a number of variations of *glissade*—they may be done back, front, under, over, forward, and backward. *Glissade* is in constant use in ballet as a connecting step between steps of high elevation. In this book we shall concern ourselves with the *glissade derrière* (back) and the *glissade devant* (front). Your teacher will give you other variations of the *glissade* as you progress in your training.

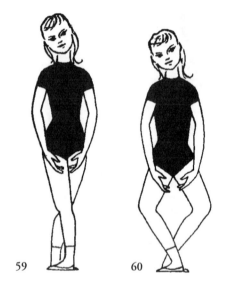

59   60

GLISSADE DERRIÈRE

59. Ready to begin. Stand in Fifth Position with the right foot front. Arms in Fifth Position, low, right shoulder slightly front, head inclined to right, eyes looking straight out.

60. *Demi-plié.* Be sure that the weight is evenly distributed over both feet, that the knees are pushed outward over the toes, and that your back is straight. Count "And."

61. Slide the left foot out to a strong point in Second Position as far as the toes can reach (don't let your hips come out of alignment!). Open the arms slightly outward. Remain in the *plié* on the supporting leg. Count "A."

62. Take a slight spring upward from the supporting foot, pointing both feet, toes grazing the floor. Open both arms outward farther to *demi-seconde* p15osition.

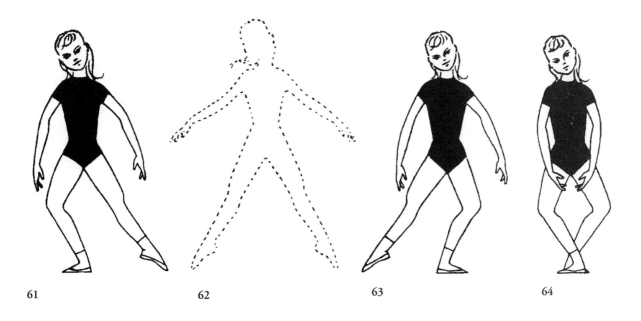

61   62   63   64

63. Transfer the weight of the body to the left foot, bending the left knee in *fondu* (roll down the foot as you *plié*). Stretch the right foot to a strong point as far as it can reach in Second Position.

64. Slide the right foot into Fifth Position in front of the left foot. Do not straight the knees, remain in the *plié*. Close the arms to Fifth Position Low. The right shoulder remains slightly forward and the head remains inclined to the right. Count "One."

You can tell from the musical counts that the movements illustrated in pictures 61 and 62 occur very quickly. Do not jerk them, just because they are fast. Try to make the whole thing very smooth.

Practice the *glissade* to a slow waltz (3/4 rhythm). The step should finish on the first beat of the measure. Take three *glissades derrière* to the left followed by one *changement*. On the *changement* turn the left shoulder slightly forward and incline the head to the left. Then repeat the whole step to the other side.

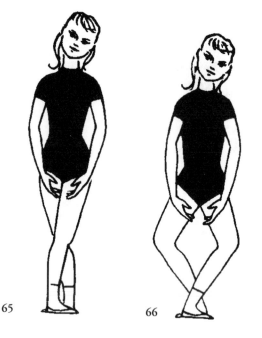

65   66

GLISSADE DEVANT

65. Ready to begin. Stand in Fifth Position with the left foot front. Arms in Fifth Position Low. Left shoulder slightly front, head inclined to the left, eyes looking straight out.

66. *Demi-plié.* Count "And."

67. Slide the left foot out to a strong point in Second

Position as far as the toes can reach. Left knee is straight, right knee remains in *plié*. Open the arms slightly outward. Count "A."

68. Take a slight spring upward through the ball of the supporting foot. Do not leave the ground but point both feet. Open both arms outward a little farther to *demi-seconde* Position.

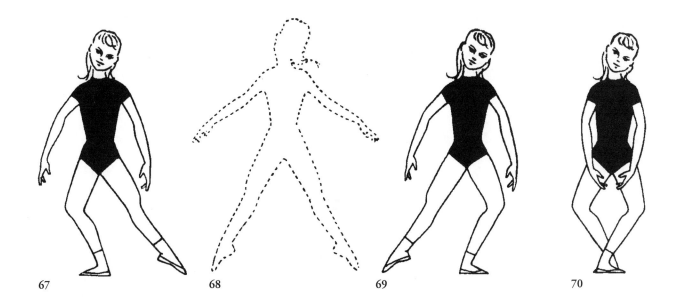

67   68   69   70

69. Transfer the weight of the body to the left foot, bending the left knee in a soft *fondu.* Stretch the right leg to a strong point as far as it can reach.

70. Slide the right foot into Fifth Position behind the left foot, remaining in the *plié.* Close the arms to Fifth Position Low. The left shoulder remains slightly forward and the head remains inclined to the left. Count "One."

Practice the *glissade devant* just as you practice the *glissade derrière.* You may also practice one *glissade* followed by one *changement* or a *jeté* or *assemblé.*

145

Assemblé

(ah-sahm-blay')

The name of this step comes from the French verb *assembler*, which means "to bring together." There are a number of variations of *assemblé*. They may be done over, under, front, behind, forward, and backward. In this book we shall concern ourselves only with the *assemblé dessus* (ah-sahm-blay' deh-su) (over) and the *assemblé dessous* (ah-sahm-blay' deh-soo') (under). Your teacher will teach you other ways to do *assemblé* as you progress in your training.

ASSEMBLÉ DESSUS, SOUTENU

An *assemblé* is said to be *soutenu* (soo-teh-nu') when the *plié* is sustained for a count and the knees straightened before taking the next step.

71. Ready to begin. Stand in Fifth Position, right foot front. Face front, look straight out. Arms in Fifth Position Low.

72. *Demi-plié* and at the same time slide the left foot out to a strong point in Second Position. Keep your back straight, don't bend forward. Take care not to sit into the supporting hip or to raise the hip on the left side. Count "And."

73. Raise the left foot slightly off the floor. Count "A."

74. Spring straight up into the air, pushing up through the ball of the right foot. Stretch your body up out of your hips, force down through the knee and toes of your right leg, stretch the left leg into a strong point. Open the arms to

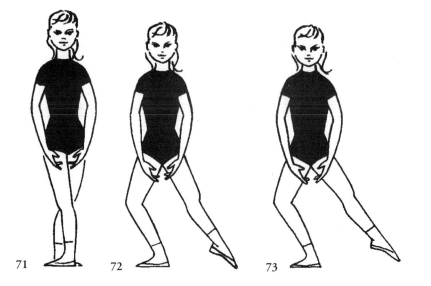

71   72   73

Position, incline the head to the left.

75. As your descend from the jump, bring the feet together into Fifth Position, in the air, with the left foot front.

76. Finish in *demi-plié* in Fifth Position with the left foot front. Both feet must touch the floor at the very same instant. Don't forget to roll down your insteps into the heels. Count "One."

77. Straighten both knees as you lower both arms to Fifth Position Low. Count "And two."

Practice this *assemblé soutenu* to a slow 3/4 rhythm. The landing from the jump should take place on the first beat of the measure and the straightening of the knees on the first beat of the

74   75   76   77

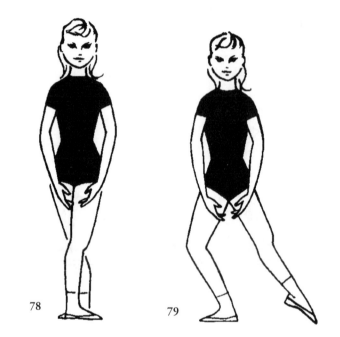

78   79

ASSEMBLÉ DESSOUS, SOUTENU

78. Ready to begin. Stand in Fifth Position, left foot front, head erect, look straight out. Arms in Fifth Position Low.

79. *Demi-plié* and at the same time slide the left foot out to a strong point in Second Position. Count "And."

80. Raise the left foot slightly off the floor. Count "A."

81. Spring straight up into the air, pushing forcefully up through the ball of the right foot. Tense both legs and point both feet hard. Open the arms to *demi-seconde* Position and incline the head to the right.

82. As your descend from the jump, bring the feet together into Fifth Position with the left foot behind.

83. Finish softly in a good *demi-plié* in Fifth Position, left foot behind. Don't forget that the toes of both feet must touch the floor at the same instant. Press both heels firmly into the floor, do not roll over onto the arches as you *plié*. Count "One."

148

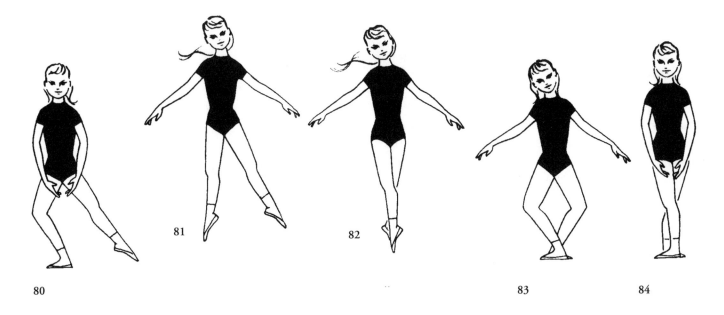

80

81

82

83

84

84. Straighten both knees as you lower both arms to Fifth Position Low. Count "And two."

Practice this *assemblé dessous* just as you practice the *assemblé dessus*, alternating left and right foot. Doing eight *assemblé dessus* will cause you to travel forward from the back of the room to the front. Doing *assemblé dessous* will cause you to travel backward from the front of the room to the back.

As you progress in your studies, you may take the *assemblé de suite* (deh su-eet'). That is, instead of straightening the knees after the *assemblé* is finished, the second *assemblé* is made from the *plié* of the first.

149

Jeté
(zheh-tay')

The name of this step comes from the French verb *jeter* which means "to fling." In this step we fling the leg out and then fall upon it. There are many kinds of *jetés*. In this book we shall concern ourselves only with the *jeté derrière* (in back) and the *jeté devant* (in front). These are also called *jeté à la seconde en avant* and *jeté à la seconde en arrière*, or *jeté* to second position traveling forward and backward. You will learn other ways to do *jeté* as you progress in your training.

Jeté Derrière

85. Ready to begin. Stand in Fifth Position, left foot front, face directly front, head erect, look straight out, arms held in d*emi-seconde* position.

86. Demi-plié and at the same time slide the right foot out to a strong point in Second Position, raising it slightly above the floor. The brush on the floor should be heard. Hold your back straight, don't bend forward. Keep the arms nicely in the *demi-seconde* position without any strain in the hands or stiffness in the elbows. Count "And."

87. Spring straight up into the air, forcing the left knee to straighten and the left foot to point downward. The right knee and foot must also be straight and point. Count "A."

85   86

88. Fall into a *demi-plié* on the right foot directly in front of the left foot. At the same time raise the left foot to a pointed position directly behind the calf of the right leg and incline the head to the right. The left foot should touch the right leg and both knees must be pushed back and out. As you fall onto the right foot, be sure to turn it out so that the heel is well forward. Remember to alight from the jump into a soft *fondu*—that is, roll down from the instep into the heel as you *plié*.

87 88 89-90 91 92

89. Repeat the *jeté* onto the left foot. Brush the left foot down and out to Second Position—touch the floor as you brush so that the sound is heard.

90. Finish the brush in a strong point in Second Position a little above the floor. Count "And."

91. Spring straight up into the air, pushing up through the ball of the right foot; stretch the knee and the toe forcefully downward into a strong point as you lift the body up out of the hips. The left knee and foot must be straight and pointed, too. Count "A."

92. Fall into a *demi-plié* on the left foot directly in front of the right foot. At the same time raise the right foot to a pointed position behind the calf of the left leg and incline the head to the left. Count "Two."

Continue to practice the *jeté derrière* alternating right and left foot eight times. This takes you in a direct line forward from the back of the room to the front. Take care that you do your brush directly to Second Position each time and that you fall directly over the supporting foot, not out to the side. Practice to a slow 2/4 rhythm, checking each landing for straight back, turned-out knees, turned-out supporting foot, heel pressed firmly into the floor, and foot straight, not rolled in on the arch.

Jeté Devant

93. Ready to begin. Stand in Fifth Position, left foot front, head erect, look straight ahead, arms held in *demi-seconde* position.

94. *Demi-plié* and at the same time slide the left foot out to a strong point in Second Position, allowing it to finish slightly above the floor. The brush on the floor should be heard. Hold your back straight, don't bend forward. Count "And."

95. Spring straight up into the air, forcing the right knee to straighten and the right foot into a strong downward point. The left knee and foot must be straight and pointed, too. Count "A."

93   94   95   96   97–98

96. Fall into a plié on the left foot directly in behind the right foot. At the same time raise the right foot to a pointed position directly in front of the left shin and incline the head to the left. Press the knees well back and out and hold the right foot close to the left leg. As you alight from the spring, be sure to use your instep and to press the left heel forward on the floor. Count "One."

97. Repeat the jeté onto the right foot. This time brush the right foot out to Second Position from its place in front of the left leg. Slide the right foot down on the floor.

98. Point the right foot strongly in Second Position a little above the floor. Count "And."

99. Spring straight up into the air, pushing up forcefully through the left foot into a strong point, lift the body well out of the hips, straighten the head. Count "A."

100. Fall into a demi-plié on the right foot directly behind the left foot. At the same time raise the left foot to a pointed position in front of the right shin and incline the head to the right. Count "Two."

Continue to practice the *jeté devant* alternating left and right foot. This takes you in a direct line backward. Take care not to jump to the side. Practice as in the *jeté derrière*.

In these *allegro* steps you can easily see how our exercises at the barre help to prepare us for their proper execution. For example, the *battement dégagé* helps us with the *échappé*, the *battement soutenu* is actually part of the step *assemblé*, and the *battement frappé* is actually part of the step *jeté*. You can begin to understand, therefore, the importance of practicing the barre exercises carefully and correctly in order to dance better.

99   100

Coupé

(coo-pay')

The name of this step comes from the French verb *couper* which means "to cut." We "cut" one foot away from the other.

There are several different ways to do this step. The coupé may be used simply as a preparation to transfer the weight from one foot to another or it may be done as a jumping step in *allegro*. Since this book deals with *allegro* steps, we shall concern ourselves with the *coupé sauté, dessous* and *dessus* (coo-pay' soh-tay', deh-soo', deh-su) (*coupé* jump, under and over).

COUPÉ DESSOUS

101. Ready to begin. Stand on the right foot with the left foot pointed behind the right heel. The body is facing *en croisé* (in this case the lower left corner of the room). Hold the right arm in Fifth Position Low, the left arm in *demi-seconde* (Cecchetti Third Position) and the head inclined to the right.

102. *Demi-plié* and raise the left foot to a pointed position in back of the right calf muscle. Count "And."

103. Spring up through the ball of the right foot, pointing the toes hard. Count "A."

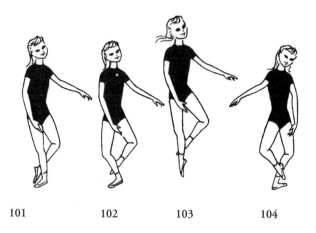

101   102   103   104

104. Fall onto the left foot directly under the right, rolling down the instep into a good *demi-plié*. At the same time raise the right foot to a pointed position in front of the left shin. As you descend, reverse the positions of the arms so that the left arm is in Fifth Position Low, the right in *demi-seconde*, and the head inclined to the left. Count "One, two."

154

COUPÉ DESSUS

105. From the position in which you have landed after taking the coupé dessous, spring up through the ball of the left foot.

106. Fall onto the right foot directly over the left foot. At the same time raise the left leg to a pointed position behind the calf muscle of the right leg. As you descend, reverse the positions of the arms and head so that the right arm is in Fifth Position Low, the left in *demi-seconde*, and the head inclined to the right. Count "Three, four."

In doing these *coupés* be sure that your knees and your supporting foot are well turned out and that you are not rolling in on your insteps in the *demi-pliés*.

Practice the *coupé*, alternating *dessous* and *dessus*, to a slow 4/4 rhythm. This is valuable practice to develop the springiness of your insteps, if you work carefully and correctly, and will develop strength in your insteps and ankles as well as good *ballon*. Take six *coupés* alternating *dessous* and *dessus*, finish with an *assemblé dessus, soutenu* (page 146). On the *assemblé* turn to face the opposite corner. Then repeat the *coupés* and the *assemblé* to the other side.

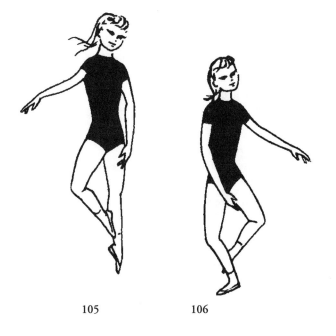

105   106

Pas de Chat

(pah deh shah')

Pas de chat in French means "step of the cat." It gets its name from the swift action of the feet like a cat's paws when it pounces upon something. *Pas de chat* may be done *petit* (small) or *grand* (big). In doing *petit pas de chat* the feet are raised only to ankle height. In doing *grand pas de chat* the feet are raised to knee height. In this book we shall concern ourselves with the *grand pas de chat*, as the *petit pas de chat* is more difficult because it requires more speed.

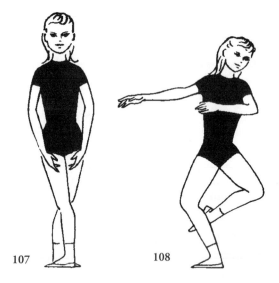

107   108

107. Ready to begin. Stand in Fifth Position, right foot front. Face directly front with the head erect and the arms in Fifth Position Low.

108. *Demi-plié* with the right leg and at the same time raise the left knee so that the left foot points behind the right knee. As you do this, raise the arms to Fourth Position Front with the left arm across the body. Bend the body a little to the left side, turning the head left to look at the left knee. Count, "And."

109. Spring up into the air, raising the right knee. Be sure that both knees are well turned out and both feet pointed.

110. Alight on the left foot, rolling down the instep into a good *demi-plié*, with the right foot strongly pointed in front of the left knee. The body remains bent to the left. Count, "A."

111. Quickly follow the left foot with the right, closing it to Fifth Position in front of the left, and remain in the *demi-plié*. Do not change the position of your body or head. Count, "One.

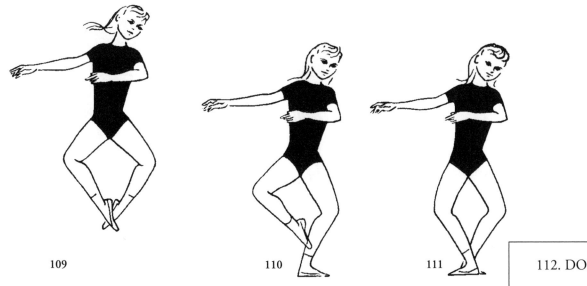

109   110   111

112. DON'T DO THIS!

112

As in all *allegro* steps take care that in alighting from the jump you do not allow your knees to fall in front of your insteps so that the arches are rolled under. Be sure that your knees are well turned out and pressed as far back as possible all through this step.

Practice the *pas de chat* to a slow 2/4 rhythm. Take three *pas de chat* to the left, followed by one *changement*. On the *changement* lower both arms to Fifth Position Low and face directly front. Then begin the *pas de chat* to the other side.

Pas de Basque, Glissé

(pah deh bahsk, glee-say')

Pas de basque gets its name from the Basque country, where France and Spain meet. *Pas* means "step"—step of the Basques. The *pas de basque* is a basic step of the folk dancing of these people. In ballet it has been adopted to be performed in two ways—*glissé*, or sliding on the floor, and *sauté*, or jumping off the floor. In this book we are concerned with the *pas de basque glissé*. The *pas de basque* may be performed *en avant* (forward) and *en arrière* (backward).

113   114   115

PAS DE BASQUE, EN AVANT

113. Ready to begin. Stand in Fifth Position with left foot front. Direction of the body is *en croisé* (here, the lower right corner of the room). Hold arms in Fifth Position Low and head inclined to the right.

114. *Demi-plié* with the right leg and slide the left foot front to a strong point in Fourth Position. Raise the arms to Second Position; the head remains inclined to the right. Count "And."

115. Describe a *demi-rond de jambe à terre*; finish with left foot strongly pointed to Second Position. Remain in *demi-plié* on right leg. Straighten head.

116. Transfer the weight from the right foot to the left with a little spring. At the same time incline the head to the left. Count "One."

117. Slide right foot into First Position, bending knee as foot slides in. Lower arms to Fifth Position Low with head remaining inclined to left. The weight is now equalized over both feet. Count "And."

118. Continue to slide the right foot, passing through Fifth Position, to Fourth Position *en croisé*. Keep the weight equalized over both feet, both heels pressed firmly on the floor, both knees bent in *demi-plié*. Bend body to left and raise arms a little.

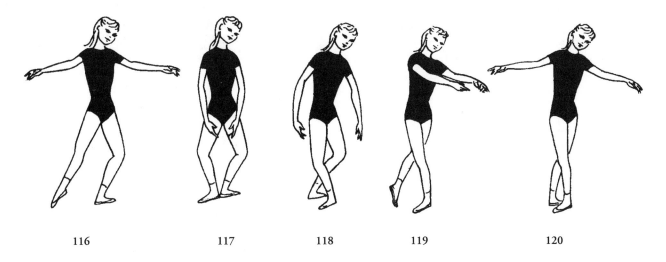

| 116 | 117 | 118 | 119 | 120 |

119. Transfer weight to right foot, straightening both knees and pointing left foot strongly in *croisé derrière* position. At the same time raise both arms to Fifth Position Front, body still inclined to left. Take care that both legs are well turned out from the hips, that the heel of the right foot is pressed forward, and that you point on the inside of the big left toe with heel pressed down. Count "Two."

120. Close the left foot behind the right into Fifth Position *demi-plié*. At the same time open both arms to Second Position. The body and head remain inclined to the left. Count "And three."

Practice the *pas de basque en avant* to a slow 3/4 rhythm (a mazurka is excellent). Alternate left and right eight times.

159

PAS DE BASQUE, EN ARRIÈRE

121. Ready to begin. Stand in Fifth Position facing straight front, right foot front. Arms in Fifth Position Low, head inclined to the right.

122. *Demi-plié* with the right leg and slide the left foot to a strong point in second, open both arms to Second Position. Count "And."

123. Transfer the weight from the right foot to the left by springing up through the ball of the right foot till both feet point, just grazing the floor, and then rolling down the left foot through the instep into a *demi-plié* with the heel pressed firmly into the floor. The right leg should be extended with straight knee to a strong point in Second Position. Head remains inclined to the right and the arms in Second Position. Count "One."

124. Slide the right foot into First Position, bending the right knee as the foot slides in. Lower the arms to Fifth Position Low; head remains inclined to the right.

125. Continue to slide the right foot back to Fourth Position *en croisé* with the weight equalized over both feet. Bend the body to the right side with the head remaining inclined to the right, and raise the arms a little. Count "And."

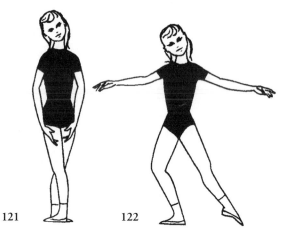

121   122

160

126. Step back onto the right foot, pointing the left foot to *croisé devant.* Raise both arms to Fifth Position Front; head and body remain inclined to the right. Count "Two."

127. Close the left foot into Fifth Position, *demi-plié,* in front of the right foot. Open both arms to Second Position, inclining the head and the body to the left side. Count "And three."

Practice the *pas de basque en arrière* eight times alternating left and right.

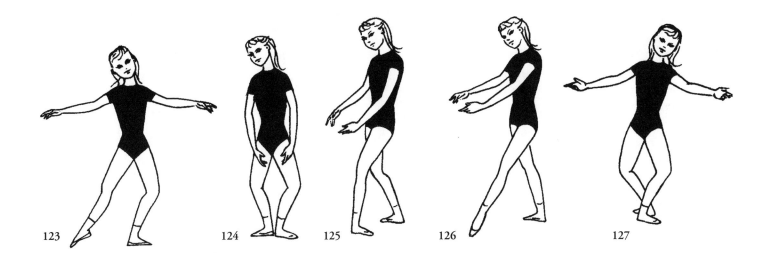

123   124   125   126   127

Chassé

(shah-say)

This step gets its name from the French verb *chasser*, which means "to chase." We "chase" one foot with the other. *Chassé* may be done forward, backward, or sideward and in any of the body positions.

In this book we shall concern ourselves only with the *chassé en avant* (*chassé* traveling forward). The direction of the body is *effacé* with the arms held in *demi-seconde*, as this is the simplest form in which to learn this step.

CHASSÉ, EN AVANT

Ready to begin. Stand in Fifth Position, left foot front, facing in the direction *effacé* (in this case the lower left corner of the room). Arms in *demi-seconde* position, head inclined to right.

128. *Demi-plié* with the weight equal over both feet. Count "And."

129. Spring straight up into the air, raising the left foot to point in front of the right ankle.

130. Alight on the right foot in *demi-plié* with the left foot pointed in front of the right instep.

131. Slide the left foot forward, throwing the weight of the body upon it, until the right leg is stretched into a strong point behind. Count "One."

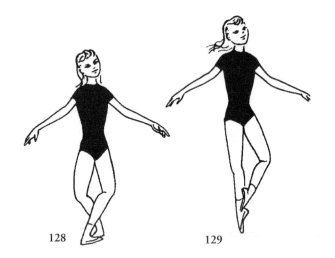

128   129

132. Draw the right foot quickly up behind the left, springing into the air with the feet pointed strongly and pressed tightly together in Fifth Position. Count "And."

162

130   131   132   133   133

133. Alight on the right foot in *demi-plié* with the left foot pointed in front of the right instep.

134. Slide the left foot forward, throwing the weight of the body upon it, until the right leg is stretched into a strong point behind. Count "Two."

Continue to practice the *chassé*, in this manner, traveling forward in a diagonal line from the upper right corner of the room to the lower left corner.

You will notice that the knees are kept straight during the jump into the air the second time. The only time the front knee bends in the air is the first time. This is as a preparation for a series of *chassés*. For all succeeding *chassés* keep both knees straight in the air.

Practice to a 6/8 rhythm played slowly so that you may think about getting everything correct. Reverse the direction of the body and practice the *chassé* the same way with the right foot front.

Pas de Bourrée

(pah de boo-ray')

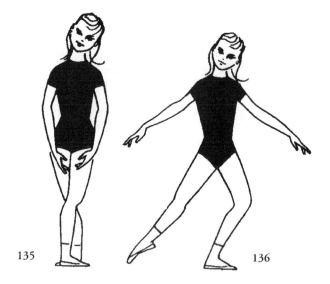

135   136

This step gets its name from a famous dance of the eighteenth century. The *bourrée* was the native dance of Auvergne, a province of France. Later this dance was adopted by the French Court. Its basic step was then adopted for use by the ballet and is known as *pas de bourrée*, or "step of the *bourrée*."

There are many variations of *pas de bourrée*. They may be done over, under, front, back, turning, changing, and without changing. In this book we concern ourselves with the *pas de bourrée dessous* (under) and *pas de bourrée dessus* (over).

The *pas de bourrée* is described in this book as it was performed in my school, the School of Ballet Repertory, in New York City. Here it is performed with a *fondu* (*plié*) on the second step. This is an old traditional way of performing this step and I prefer it because it gives great lightness to the step as well as smoothness. Practicing it in this manner develops excellent control of the feet and insteps. If this is different than the way your teacher teaches it, do not worry over it but try to learn it both ways.

PAS DE BOURRÉE DESSOUS

135. Ready to begin. Stand in Fifth Position, left foot front, left shoulder slightly front, head inclined to the left, and the arms in Fifth Position Low.

136. *Demi-plié* and slide the right foot out to a strong point in Second Position slightly above the floor. At the same time raise both arms to *demi-seconde* position. (Back straight, shoulder pulled down, body well lifted out of hips!) Count "And."

137. Rise up on the *demi-pointe* of the left foot and at the same time bring the right foot into Fifth Position on

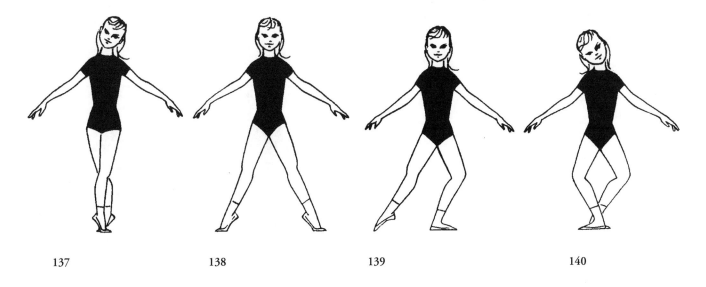

137   138   139   140

the *demi-pointe* behind the left with both knees pulled up tight. Count "One."

138. Step to Second Position on the *demi-pointe* with the left foot so that you are standing with the weight equal over both feet. Bring the head erect, look straight front.

139. Lower the left heel to the floor in *demi-plié*. At the same time stretch the right leg into a strong point in Second Position, toes touching the floor. Lower the arms slightly. This action takes place at the instant that you step on the foot in Second Position. Count "And."

140. Slide the right foot into Fifth Position in front of the left foot. Remain in the *plié*. Bring the right shoulder slightly forward and incline the head to the right as the foot slides in. Count "Two."

Do not straighten the knees before beginning the *pas de bourrée* to the other side; *dégagé* the left foot *à la seconde* while remaining in the *plié*.

Practice the *pas de bourrée* alternating right and left. If you practice with music, use a slow 4/4 rhythm, count "And one, and two, and three, and four." The preparatory brush then is done on count "Four."

165

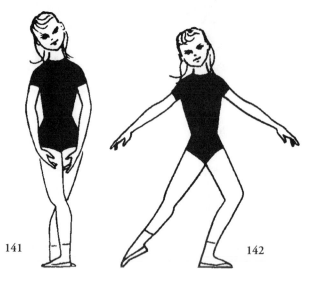

141   142

PAS DE BOURRÉE DESSUS

The *pas de bourrée dessus* differs from the *pas de bourrée dessous* in that the foot crosses over in the front rather than under in the back.

141. Ready to begin. Stand in Fifth Position with the right foot front, right shoulder slightly front, head inclined to the right, and the arms in Fifth Position Low.

142. *Demi-plié* and slide the right foot out to a strong point in Second Position slightly above the floor. At the same time raise both arms to *demi-seconde* Position. Remember that you must not permit the knee to fall in front of the arch; press it back over the toes. Count "And."

143. Rise up on the *demi-pointe* of the left foot and at the same time bring the right foot into Fifth Position on the *demi-pointe* in front of the left. Pull both knees up tight. Count "One."

144. Step to Second Position on the *demi-pointe* with the left foot. Bring the head erect and look straight out.

143   144   145   146

145. Lower the left heel to the ground in *plié*. At the same time stretch the right leg to a strong point in Second Position, toes touching the floor, and lower the arms a little. This action takes place at the instant that you step to Second Position. Count "And."

146. Slide the right foot into Fifth Position in back of the left, remaining in the *plié*. Bring the left shoulder slightly forward and incline the head to the left; lower the arms to Fifth Position Low. Count "Two."

Practice the *pas de bourrée dessus* the same way you practice the *pas de bourrée dessous*, alternating right and left.

Balancé

(bah-lahn-say')

This step gets its name from the French verb *balancer*, which means "to sway." In this step we may sway from side to side or from front to back. We shall practice it from side to side.

147. Ready to begin. Stand in Fifth Position with the right foot front, face front, head erect, looking straight out. Arms in Fifth Position Low.

148. *Demi-plié* and slide the left foot out to a strong point in Second Position a little above the floor. Raise both arms to Fifth Position Front.

149. Transfer the weight to the left foot with a little spring by using your insteps (push up through the right foot, roll down through the left foot) falling into a *demi-plié*. Open both arms halfway out to Second Position. Count "One."

147   148

150. Bring the right foot behind the left foot slightly off the floor.

151. Transfer the weight to the ball of the right foot, straightening the right knee and lifting the left foot very slightly off the floor. Count "Two.

152. Fall on the left foot, rolling down the instep into a *demi-plié*, and raise the right foot very slightly off the floor behind the left foot. At the same time lower the arms to Fifth Position Low. Count "Three."

Repeat the three counts to the right side. Practice the *balancé* to a slow waltz (3/4 rhythm). Alternate left and right sixteen times. Practice it holding the arms in Fifth Position Low, until you have the feet well under control, then add the *port de bras*. Your teacher will teach you other ways to use the arms as you progress in your training.

149   150   151   152

Sissonne (Fermée)

(see-sohn' fehr-may')

This step gets its name from the dancer who invented it. There are many different kinds of *sissonnes*. They may be done closed, open, over, under, changing, without changing, forward, backward, and sideward. They may be done in any of the body positions such as *croisé*, *écarté*, and *effacé*, in any of the *arabesque* positions, and with a variety of *port de bras*. In the Russian school the *temps levé* from two feet to one foot is called a "*sissonne simple.*"

We are concerned with the *sissonne fermée, en avant* and *en arrière* (*sissonne* closed, forward and backward). These may be done traveling from the back of the room to the front and vice versa, or they may be taken traveling on a diagonal line from corner to corner.

SISSONNE FERMÉE, EN AVANT

The *sissonne fermée, en avant,* is here described taken on a diagonal line from the upper right corner of the room to the lower left corner (direction is *effacé*) with the arms in the First Arabesque position.

153. Ready to begin. Stand in Fifth Position with the left foot front. Face the lower left corner of the room. Head erect, look straight ahead, arms in Fifth Position Low.
154. *Demi-plié* with both legs.

153   154   155

155. Spring forward into the air, taking the right leg back to Fourth Position in the air, point both feet strongly, and force both knees to straighten. At the same time open both arms outward. Count "And."

170

156   157   158

Practice eight *sissonnes* in this manner, traveling always toward the lower left corner. Then repeat on the other foot, traveling on the diagonal from the upper left corner to the lower right. Practice to a slow waltz (3/4) rhythm. The closing after the spring takes place on the first beat of the measure and the second two beats are held in the *plié* position. The next *sissonne* takes its spring from this *plié*. You may practice this step with the arms held in Fifth Position Low until you have control of the feet and legs. You may also practice it with the arms held in First Arabesque position throughout without raising and lowering them each time. As you progress in your studies, add the *port de bras*.

156. Alight softly on the left foot in *fondu* (roll down the instep into a *plié*) with the arms in First Arabesque position. Hold the good lift out of the hips and keep your back straight and strong with the shoulder blades well pulled down. Count "A."

157. Touch the floor in Fourth Position Back with the toes of the right foot.

158. Slide the right foot into Fifth Position behind the left, maintaining the *plié*. Lower the arms to Fifth Position Low. Count, "One."

159. DON'T DO THIS!

In practicing this step take great care that your body does not bend forward (break) as you alight from the spring. You must keep a good lift out of the hips and with the ribs, both in the air and on the floor, otherwise the step will give the appearance of being labored and heavy instead of easy and light.

159

SISSONNE FERMÉE, EN ARRIÈRE

The *sissonne fermée, en arrière,* is here described taken on a diagonal line from the lower right corner to the upper left (direction *effacé*) with the arms in *effacé* position.

160. Ready to begin. Stand in Fifth Position with the right foot front. Face the lower right corner of the room. Head erect, look straight ahead. Arms in Fifth Position Low.

161. *Demi-plié* with both legs and raise the arms to Fifth Position in front.

162. Spring backward, taking the right leg front to Fourth Position in the air, and open the arms to Third Position with the left arm up. At the same time incline the head to the left and look out to the audience. Point both feet strongly and force both knees to straighten. Count "And."

163. Come down softly on the left foot in *fondu* (roll down into a *demi-plié*), maintaining the *effacé* position of the arms and head.

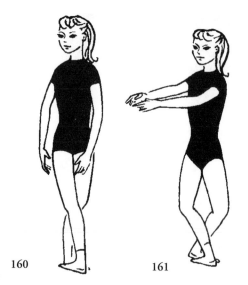

160   161

164. Touch the floor with the toes of your right foot.

165. Slide the right foot into Fifth Position in front of the left foot, maintaining the *plié*. The arms and head remain in the *effacé* position. Count "One."

172

162   163   164   165

Practice this step exactly as I have described the practice for the *sissonne* traveling forward. Maintain the arms in the *effacé* position throughout once you have raised them to this position. For preliminary practice it is wise not to use the arms but to maintain them in the Fifth Position Low until you have acquired the necessary skill with the legs and feet. Take care that you do not allow the open leg to fly up too high as you alight from the spring, but maintain strong control of your hips and back.

About the Author
Thalia Mara

Thalia gave the gift of life, light and love to everyone and everything she touched. Thalia's life was one of celebration, and we should all be grateful that she happened our way.

Governor of Mississippi Ronnie Musgrove (November 2003)

Thalia Mara, Founder and Artistic Director of the USA International Ballet Competition, believed that dance is life, retirement is death, and that the arts must be offered as basic education in any great civilization.

Mara's successes reflected her inexhaustible talent, driving work ethic and eloquence in inspiring artistic collaboration. She was equally cherished by family and friends for her spiritual generosity, wisdom, intellect, self-effacing storytelling and humor.

Thalia Mara was born Elizabeth Simmons in Chicago in 1911, the daughter of Russian immigrants (who had changed their name from Semyonov). She made her ballet debut on a vaudeville stage at the age of eleven and by fourteen was a full member of the Chicago Opera Ballet under the direction of Adolph Bolm.

Because an American ballet tradition had not yet developed in the 1920s, Thalia went to Paris at the age of sixteen to learn ballet at its source, studying with the legendary Nicholas Legat and Olga Preobrajenska. She soon rose to prominence as a soloist with the Ballet Suedois and L'Opera Privé de Paris, where she danced under the direction of the great master Fokine. She performed in one of the first performances of his immortal opera ballet, *Prince Igor*.

Thalia came back to America to the depths of the Great Depression. In New York, she found a job with the Chester Hale Dancers, performing four shows a day (five on holidays), dancing ballet, jazz, tap, character dancing, ballet on roller skates, and on a tiny platform suspended from the Chrysler Building, 57 stories above the street. She danced at the opening of Radio City Music Hall and on Broadway. She changed her name to *Thalia* (the Greek muse of humor) *Mara* (a family name) to attract more stage work. Fortunately, she reunited with Fokine, becoming a soloist in New York's Fokine Ballet.

Mara married dancer and choreographer Arthur Mahoney, who she had met in Paris. The two toured the U.S. as concert artists, then began teaching in New York in the early 1940s. Thus began the career of one of the greatest American ballet educators —Thalia Mara went on to have in international reputation, influencing generations of dancers.

Mara and Mahoney founded the School of Dance Arts at Carnegie Hall, and three years later the professional School of Ballet Repertory, which thrived for sixteen years. They also served as directors of Jacob's Pillow, where among the faculty they hired was Joseph Pilates, who taught exercises to dancers. From 1952 to 1963, Thalia served a president of the Ballet Repertory Guild, a teaching and certifying organization for ballet teachers that had the mission of setting standards for dance teaching in America. She taught at New York's High School of Performing Arts, then in 1963 founded and directed the National Academy of Ballet, where elementary and high school students received a complete education with extensive training in the performing arts. She wrote a dozen books, including several ballet textbooks that were published in the United States and England and translated in German, Spanish, Arabic and Japanese.

In 1976, when Thalia Mara was 65, an age when most people retire, she moved to Jackson, Mississippi, taking with her a dream that the capital city could become an arts center for the deep South. She was indomitable when implementing a vision that adhered to the "rightness" it espoused. By 1979, she had made the Jackson Ballet a fully professional company of 24 dancers and a performing member of the Southeastern Regional Ballet Association. In 1979, the Mara dream became a reality when Jackson was host of the first International Ballet Competition (IBC) in the western hemisphere. She served as artistic director through the fifth IBC, in 1994, having guided the sold-out competition into what many considered the world's best. The IBC continues in Jackson and rotates annually to other cities in the world; its home in Jackson is Thalia Mara Hall, formerly the city's Municipal Auditorium. At the 2002 IBC, the audience cheered when leaders presented her with a gold medal for lifetime achievement in the arts. The honor was one of many lifetime and arts achievement awards, including those from the governor of Mississippi, the Mayor of Jackson, the Professional Dance Teachers Association, the Polish Government (the Vaslav Nijinsky Medal of Honor) and from the Mississippi Historical Society (the Award of Merit for Outstanding Contribution to Mississippi).

She founded the nonprofit Thalia Mara Arts International Foundation in 1991, which has sponsored the celebration of Mississippi's 175th year of statehood, scholarships for teacher training at the IBC's dance school, a city-wide French course for children and the 1997 Yamaha International Piano Competition. Since 1999, the foundation, through its World Performance Series, has brought performances to Mississippi that continue to expose its citizens to the highest standard of art. They include the American Ballet Theatre, the Alvin Ailey American Dance Theatre, violinist Joshua Bell, Dance Theatre of Harlem, bluesman B.B. King and virtuoso Wynton Marsalis and the Lincoln Center Jazz Orchestra.

During her Jackson career, Mara was a guest teacher for many U.S. ballet companies and workshops and served as a consultant and jurist for the first Alicia Alonso International Dance Competition in Havana, the International Concours de Ballet in Tokyo, the Japan Ballet and Modern Dance Competition in Nagoya, the National Ballet Company of Egypt and the Mexican National Ballet.

Thalia Mara thought it was important to hold beauty close to one's experience; that without maintaining a keen sense of what real beauty is, our society would fail. Even more important, however, is holding to the highest standards one of capable of achieving. Thalia Mara died in Jackson at the age of 92 in October, 2003, leaving behind legions of people who had the highest regard for her as a person, a friend and a professional.

Other Books and Videos from Princeton Book Company, Publishers, for students and parents

Bibliography

Whitehill, Angela and William Noble. *The Parents Book of Ballet: Answers to Critical Questions About the Care and Development of Young Dancers, 2nd Edition.*

_____. *The Nutcracker Backstage: The Story and The Magic.*

Lihs, Harriet R. *Appreciating Dance: A Guide to the World's Liveliest Art, 3rd Edition.*

Newman, Barbara. *Sadler's Wells Royal Ballet Swan Lake.* London: Dance Books Ltd.

Harrison, Mary Kent. *How to Dress Dancers: Costuming Techniques for Dance.*

Mara, Thalia. *The Language of Ballet: A Dictionary.*

Spilken, Terry L., M.D. *The Dancer's Foot Book.*

Chmelar, Robin and Sally S. Fitt. *Diet for Dancers: A Complete Guide to Nutrition and Weight Control.*

Videography

Ballet 101 Series:
Ballet 101; Ballet 201; Ballet 101 & 201, Combinations 1; Ballet 101 & 201, Combinations 2. With Angela Russ; based on the syllabus of the University of California at Irvine
each approx. 50 minutes, color.

Zena Rommett Floor-Barre & Ballet Technique for Young Dancers with Sarah Cunningham
35 minutes, color.

My First Pointe Shoes with Michelle Benash
25 minutes, color.

Simply Ballet: An Easy-to-Follow Class for Beginners with Michelle Benash
55 minutes, color.

Ballet Class for Beginners with David Howard
40 minutes, color.

Step into Ballet with Wayne Sleep of the Royal Ballet
50 minutes, color.

Videography (continued)

The Children of Theatre Street (The Kirov Ballet School)
narrated by Princess Grace of Monaco
92 minutes, color.

Cinderella, A Ballet in Three Acts
with Antoinette Sibley, Anthony Dowell and the Royal Ballet
Choreography by Ashton, Music by Prokofiev
102 minutes, color.

The Nutcracker
with Ekaterina Maximova, Vladimir Vasiliev and The Bolshoi Ballet
Choreography by Grigorovich, Music by Tchaikovsky
100 minutes, color.

The Nutcracker
with Merle Park, Rudolf Nureyev and The Royal Ballet
Choreography by Nureyev, Music by Tchaikovsky
100 minutes, color.

The Sleeping Beauty, A Ballet in Three Acts
with Viviana Durante, Anthony Dowell and
The Royal Ballet Covent Garden
Choreography by Petipa, Ashton and MacMillan, Music by Tchaikovsky
132 minutes, color.

The Sleeping Beauty
with Christine Walsh, David Ashmole and The Australian Ballet
Choreography by Petipa, Music by Tchaikovsky
134 minutes, color.

The Sleeping Beauty
with Altynai Asylmuratova, Konstantin Zaklinsky and The Kirov Ballet
Choreography by Petipa, Music by Tchaikovsky
160 minutes, color.

I'm A Ballerina Now with Rosemary Boross
and students of the Red Bank Dance Academy
40 minutes, color.

DVDs

Cinderella, A Ballet in Three Acts
with Antoinette Sibley, Anthony Dowell and the Royal Ballet
Choreography by Ashton, Music by Prokofiev
102 minutes, color.

The Nutcracker
with Maximova, Vasiliev and The Bolshoi Ballet
Choreography by Grigorovich, Music by Tchaikovsky
100 minutes, color.

The Sleeping Beauty, A Ballet in Three Acts
with Durante, Dowell and The Royal Ballet Covent Garden
Choreography by Petipa, Ashton and Macmillan, Music by Tchaikovsky.

Compact Disc

Music for Ballet Class with Olga Meyer, Pianist